# Vlogg

# Viral Marketing

# And

# Laptop Lifestyle

Use the Power of Video and Virality to Grow
Your Online Brand and Attract the Right
Audience While Living Like a Digital Nomad
and Enjoying the Freedom

By Adam Torbert

# Contents

Thank you for buying this book and I hope that you will find it useful. If you will want to share your thoughts on this book, you can do so by leaving a review on the Amazon page, it helps me out a lot.

# Vlogging

## Learn How to Use the Power of Video to Successfully Grow Your Online Following and Make a Profit

By Adam Torbert

# Introduction to Vlogging

Vlogging is ending up being progressively more prominent and there has actually never ever been a greater time to begin a vlog. Individuals truly delight in viewing top quality vlogs and certain vloggers have millions of subscribers. However, you do not require countless subscribers to generate income from vlogging. There are lots of vloggers who have a good deal less subscribers which make full-time earnings and more from their vlogging endeavors. What might be better? Doing something that you like and capturing it to show the world and generating income simultaneously. This is more than a dream-- it could be your truth if you adhere to the recommendations offered within this guide.

Within this book, you are going to find what a vlog truly is, some terrific and lucrative ideas for beginning a vlog, how to begin your brand-new vlog with optimal impact and how to advertise your vlog so that you boost your subscriber count and your capacity to generate income.

I have actually responded to all of the most typical concerns about vlogging within this guide and supplied you with a step by step strategy to produce an effective and successful vlog. You have to act and be absolutely devoted to your brand-new vlog. It will require some time and work to get where you wish to be.

I have actually left no stone unturned within this book. You are going to understand precisely what is expected of you and the ins and outs of vlogging. Consistency is all when it comes to vlogging as you are going to uncover as you go through this book.

As soon as you have actually checked out the guide, you are going to have all that you require to begin your journey to effective vlogging. So I suggest that you read this book completely first and after that return to the beginning and follow the advised action steps.

# Chapter 1: What is Vlogging

A video blog (vlog) or "vlogging" is the establishing of a particular channel on a video sharing website like YouTube and submitting videos regularly. The objective of your vlog is to supply appealing material in a particular niche which is going to produce a response from viewers and expand your subscriber base or following. Vlogging blasted off around 10 years back when video sharing websites such as YouTube ended up being truly popular. Videos are a great deal more fascinating than text-based material. Many folks would sooner view a brief video than check out numerous words of text.

Could vlogging actually make you cash? Yes, it definitely can, however, you have to handle it in the proper way, which is what this manual is all about. You are going to see how to select a specific niche to vlog about, the most effective video platform to utilize, how to establish your channel properly and a whole lot more.

## Why Should You Start a Vlog?

There are lots of excellent reasons why you ought to begin a vlog today. The very first of these is that video has a significant impact nowadays. Facebook and YouTube presently control the world of Web video. There is a reason why both of these networks launched live streaming video-- it is what individuals desire! Individuals like to see videos and specifically, they like vlogs. A few of the most prosperous channels on YouTube are vlogs. When you begin to get a following for your vlog, the word is going to spread rapidly and you are going to get a great deal more subscribers.

Vlogging is among the ideal methods for you to share your skills, thoughts and ideas about a topic. When you develop a vlog your audience is not expecting Hollywood film quality-- actually, quite the opposite. A vlog has to be genuine and informal and truly relate to the audience.

There are all sorts of effective vlogs available. A great deal of travel vlogs make it possible for the vloggers to travel around the globe through contributions, sponsorship, affiliate marketing and various other income possibilities. Have a look at the appeal of reality TV-- individuals like to see other regular folks doing things that they enjoy.

In case you have a particular skill, then you can demonstrate to the world how you put this to excellent use. As soon as you begin to develop a following, then there are going to be possibilities for you to market your abilities. By showing that you are actually proficient at something in your vlog, you are bound to get demands from individuals thinking about hiring you.

Certain individuals begin a vlog since they wish to record their life and develop a memory to show future generations. They have no monetary goals for doing so. This is a book about generating income from vlogging, so I would not suggest this technique. Nevertheless, a variety of vloggers who began by doing this have actually made passive income.

There are currently some really prosperous vloggers on YouTube who earn a substantial profit from their vlog. Individuals such as  Lilly Singh, Roman

Attwood, Zoella, Casey Neistat, and Alfie Deyes are all fine examples.

These individuals all have deals with brand names where they earn a considerable profit. Brands continuously search YouTube for brand-new vloggers and in case they discover good ones, they are going to approach them straight with offers or sponsorship. There are numerous possibilities to generate income with vlogging.

You could begin vlogging today. There is no requirement for you to acquire costly camera equipment initially. If you have a mobile phone that could capture top-quality video, then you are good to go. Nevertheless, in case you can buy great recording devices, I would usually advise this.

When you have actually wrapped up shooting your video footage, you could then transfer this to your computer system and utilize cost-free video editing software like Windows Movie Maker for Windows devices or iMovie for Mac. Yes, there are superior video editors available, however, you do not require them to get going.

You do not even require a site. Utilize YouTube as your vlogging platform. It is a great idea to have social profiles like Facebook, Twitter and Instagram and construct a following on these so that you could allow everybody to know when you have actually released a fresh video.

A variety of vloggers utilize affiliate marketing to produce revenue. For instance, there are a variety of effective makeup and cosmetics vlogs and the owners advertise items and earn commissions as an affiliate.

## What Should your Vlog Be About ?

The primary guideline with developing a vlog is to make it about anything which you are truly intrigued by. There are no set guidelines here-- you can actually develop a vlog about anything. However, I would recommend that you comply with the actions listed beneath to recognize a truly excellent vlogging topic:

1. Compose a list of the things which truly intrigue you in life. Incorporate everything here like things which you delight in doing at work, in your free time, with your buddies, and so on.

2. Compose a second list of the skills that you possess. Do not even believe that you have no skills-- you are going to be proficient at some things for certain.

3. Take a look at these lists and consider the business possibilities with each interest and skill. In case you are a sports fan, for instance, and follow a specific team, in that case, is there an opportunity available for you? Certain sports vlog owners are rich!

4. Utilize the Google Keyword Planner to assess and see the number of searches per month that exist for your passions and skills. You could likewise browse on YouTube to see which videos show up and the number of subscribers and views they have.

5. Select your vlogging subject based upon the most effective blend of interest or skills and business possibilities. The majority of vlogging guides are going to inform you to simply vlog about something which you are passionate about. You are going to definitely want to be enthusiastic about your vlogging, yet not all topics have the very same lucrative potential.

6. As soon as you have actually picked a vlogging topic or niche, you are going to have to assess to see if you can produce lots of videos with it. Individuals are going to want you to vlog typically-- you can't simply submit one video and expect wonders. So is there ample material for you to develop a weekly or month-to-month vlog? In the following chapter, you are going to discover some terrific ideas for beginning a rewarding vlog.

**The Benefits of Starting a Vlog**

There are a variety of benefits of a vlog over a basic blog site. The primary reason because of which individuals choose to produce basic blog sites is that it is much easier than producing a vlog. You could compose a post for a basic blog site relatively quickly or outsource it to an expert writer. However, it is unsurprising that individuals choose video.

With a basic blog site it is really challenging to establish a following. Ranking blog sites in the search engines is truly hard nowadays, and there are individuals promoting various blog sites all across social networks. The competition is harsh. Indeed there is competition in vlogging, however, it is a lot less extreme.

- Individuals Vlog for more visibility-- it is simpler to get visitors to a vlog than it is to a basic blog site.

- Videos have a better chance of going viral-- you have a lot better odds of one of your vlog videos going viral than a basic article.

- Videos are more involved-- it is simpler to encourage individuals to do something with a video than it is with a composed article. You are going to be a lot more probable to attain greater conversion rates with excellent videos.

- Video Tutorials are truly powerful-- individuals like to understand how to do particular things. In case you can demonstrate to them how to attain something with a video tutorial, then this is even more fascinating than them needing to read a lengthy article with screenshots.

- You can Vlog Live-- with the live streaming functionalities of Facebook and YouTube, you can produce some videos live. In case you have an essential statement to make, then inform individuals that there will be a live stream on a particular day and at a specific time. Individuals actually enjoy live-streaming video!

- There are a variety of revenue-generating options-- from the YouTube Partnership Program to sponsorship, exclusive deals with brand names and affiliate marketing. Prominent vlogs have numerous choices when it concerns generating income.

You want to be truly dedicated to your vlog. If you invest a couple of months adding videos to your channel and after that quit, for a while, individuals are going to forget you quickly. This suggests that you are going to have lost time and work for nothing.

In case you select a topic for vlogging and there are various vloggers on YouTube in the equivalent niche, then don't allow this to put you off. Keep in mind that you are the topic of your vlog. You are different from other vloggers with your distinct individuality.

## Chapter 2: Ideas for Successful Vlogs

It could be hard to come up with that winning idea for a vlog which is going to make you substantial revenue. So to assist you, here are some excellent ideas for you within this chapter. I hope that you discover an idea here which you are able to run with.

## Video Games

Are you somebody who takes pleasure in playing video games a great deal? There are numerous individuals who play video games nowadays, and there is constantly space for another fantastic vlog on the topic. New video games show up constantly, and with the increase in appeal of Amazon's Twitch.tv there is a lot of potential for you to develop excellent videos. The trick to an effective video game vlog is supplying the video gaming community with what they desire. If they delight in the videos you produce, then they are going to get the word out for you and your vlog is going to grow tremendously. Here are a few ideas for videos you can produce:

- You playing a particular video game and beating a level or defeating a boss.

- A live stream regarding a specific video game

- A review of a video game.

- Your top 10 video games.

- Develop a video game walkthrough.

- Offer video gaming news.

## Tutorials or How-To Videos

A great deal of individuals browse YouTube to discover how to perform something. So do you have a specific set of abilities or are you a pro in a specific topic? If so, a series of "how-to" videos might be an excellent vlogging idea for you. Individuals are constantly utilizing the Web to pose questions, and videos are by far the most prominent medium which individuals select to get the responses which they require. There are simply limitless possibilities for " how-to" video tutorials. You could certainly advertise affiliate items or offer your own items on the back of a vlog this way. Here are a few ideas:

- How to construct something.

- How to generate income online.

- Life abilities.

- Personal growth abilities.

- How to get a girlfriend/boyfriend and subsequent relationship tips.

- Discover a brand-new language.

- How to secure that brand-new job and maintain it.

- How to generate income in stocks, forex and so on.

## Computer systems and Technology

Do you like computer systems and tech devices? Are you an expert on mobile phones? There are a lot of individuals that simply like computer systems and tech and would be thrilled to discover what is ensuing and so on. The world of innovation alters constantly, so you are never going to ever lack video ideas. Here are several great ideas:

- Beneficial apps for your mobile phone.

- The most effective laptop computers.

- How to utilize prominent software applications like Microsoft Office.

- Fresh technology reviews.

- Technology item comparisons.

- Computer system hacks and unfamiliar shortcuts.

- Create your personal site.

- Registering a domain name.

- How to make your computer system quicker.

- How to repair typical computer issues.

## Weight Loss and Fitness

Do you have an understanding about how to slim down and maintain the weight off? Are you a fitness pro? The need for "how-to" videos within this area is big. And the topic is so huge that you ought to never ever lack new video ideas. Here are several ideas to consider:

- Weight loss pointers

- Compare prominent diet plans e.g. Paleo, Keto and so on

- Healthy dietary dishes.

- How to stay away from food and drinks which are going to make you put on weight.

- Working out for novices.

- How to perform a workout appropriately e.g. push-ups.

- How to get in shape and shredded without heading to the fitness center.

- The advantages of yoga.

- Particular yoga workouts.

## Personal Growth

This is another big topic. Individuals constantly wish to enrich their lives and in case you have the understanding to aid them to accomplish this, then it can unlock all types of doors. Here are several terrific video ideas:

- X ways to be more positive.

- How to conquer your worries.

- How to get out of your comfort zone.

- How to establish goals and accomplish them.

- How to boost your self-confidence.

- How to be a terrific communicator.

- How to encourage individuals to perform anything.

- How to utilize NLP to alter your life.

- How to quit living in the past.

## Travel

Do you enjoy taking a trip? Have you been, or intend to go, on a journey all around the world? Can you offer suggestions for the best things to do in well-liked nations and cities? Do you wish to spend your life traveling the globe and taking pleasure in fresh experiences? A lot of other folks do too! It holds true that there are currently a great deal of travel vlogs out there; however, there is constantly space for more. Simply do something different from others. Here are a couple of ideas:

- Awesome locations you won't have visited.

- The expert guide to trendy tourist destinations.

- Locating those separated beaches.

- How to get by in a certain [place] - The leading 10 locations you need to go to.

- The ideal method to pack a traveling bag.

- Traveling on a budget.

## Music

Are you a performer? Can you show individuals how to play an instrument or how to sing effectively? Do you understand a great deal about retro music? Music is big on YouTube and excellent "how-to" videos are constantly prominent. Here are several ideas:

- How to operate the guitar.

- How to perform with the drums.

- How to repair a damaged instrument.

- The most effective guitars (or whichever instrument).

- How to read and compose music.

- Popular track covers.

- How to compose terrific lyrics.

- The greatest bands of a category, a year etc. - How to utilize an audio editor to blend the music.

- Music tools reviews.

## Pets

A few of the most prominent YouTube videos have to do with pets. Everybody has actually seen an amusing cat video or a dog carrying out unique tricks. There are lots of animal enthusiasts worldwide and they just cannot get enough material about pets. Here are several fantastic video ideas:

- How to look after your pet.

- How to instruct your dog-- numerous possibilities here.

- How to instruct your cat/dog to perform tricks.

- The ideal clothing for your cat/dog.

- The most effective names for your fresh pet.

- The ideal accessories for your pet.

- How to brush your pet.

- Unusual pets.

- Taking a trip with your pet.

- The most suitable meals for your pet.


**Beauty**


Are you somebody who understands how to use makeup properly? Are you in touch with all the most recent trends? Can you offer suggestions and recommendations for softer and cleaner skin? This marketplace is huge and the need for information is going to constantly exist. Here are several terrific video ideas:

- Various makeup tutorials.

- How to make your skin appear more youthful.

- How to look after your hair.

- The ideal clothing for the bigger individual.

- The current style accessories you need to have.

- How to select the ideal attire for the event.

- The very best shoes for ladies.

- The current style trends.

- How to appear spectacular on a budget.

## Cooking, Recipes and Food

Can you show individuals how to cook? Can you demonstrate to them how to make excellent tasting dishes? Do you have excellent recipes to impart? Do you understand the very best dining establishments? Can you inform individuals what to eat when they go to particular states or cities? Food is a big topic and constantly sought after. Here are several remarkable video ideas:

- How to prepare [something] - The best meals in a certain area - The leading 10 restaurants in a certain place - How to create healthy treats.

- The ideal foods for slimming down.

- Tropical cooking.

- The essential kitchen tools.

- How to put together food effectively.

- How to bake the best cakes.

- Meals that are going to thrill your household.

- What to eat whenever you are going to a certain city.


I hope that you find these ideas motivating. Producing a vlog which contains "how-to" videos is an excellent way to go, and you are going to have the ability to generate income from it in a variety of various methods. This is not a comprehensive list whatsoever, so have a good look at what you understand and establish a strategy for your vlog.

## Chapter 3: Launching a Prosperous Vlog

An effective vlog is going to need a little bit of preparation. Sure, you can simply head out there with your mobile phone and begin recording video footage about your enthusiasm. However, it is much better to spend some time to consider the kind of material that you wish to show individuals and where you are going to share it.

## What is the Aim of Your Vlog?

It is an excellent idea to specify the objective of your vlog. It is not an excellent idea to put in 6 months doing so! So think of your vlog as a means for you to interact with your target market. What is the general story that you wish to depict here? Here are several examples:

- I am going to take you to travel locations, which you will not believe.

- I am going to demonstrate to you how to quickly generate income on the internet from home.

- I am going to demonstrate to you how to appear stunning each day on a budget plan.

- I am going to deliver all the current updates and fan responses for a certain sports team.

Do you understand? Excellent. You wish to make your vlog stand apart from the rest. Have a look at a number of the existing vlogs on the market which have a big subscriber base for motivation. Just do not devote too much time doing this!

## Pick Your Vlogging Style

The moment you are starting with vlogging, it is ideal to perform what you are comfy with. You are going to want to reveal your face on camera-- there is no sidestepping this. Viewers are not going to be thrilled if they never ever see you in the videos. It is going to assist in driving engagement. There are various kinds of vloggers. Some are going to wish to involve their partner, their kids, their buddies, their pets etc. in their vlogs. A great deal of vloggers are going to record video footage when they are outdoors doing something. Others are going to utilize their office or home for their vlogging. Will you film all of the video footage on your own, or will another person aid you? In case you will film the video footage yourself and intend to perform this outside as you are walking around, you can utilize particular tools to accomplish this.

Are you generally funny? If so then constantly infuse some humor into your vlog. Consider other manners in which you could keep viewers amused. Making errors with vlogging is fantastic due to the fact that you can reveal the outtakes of when things failed. So think of the design you are going to utilize for your vlog. How could you make your personality actually radiate through and keep individuals involved and desiring more videos?

**What are Other Vloggers Doing?**

In case there is competition for your vlogging niche, go and have a look at what your rivals are doing. Spend some time to see their videos and discover what they do. Begin with the most prominent vlogs and work your way down. Here are several things to keep an eye out for:

- What are the topics of their videos?

- Which of their videos are the most well-known and for what reason?

- What is the typical duration of their videos?

- What engagement strategies do they utilize?

- Do they have sponsors or endorse affiliate items?

- How frequently do they post fresh videos?

In the event that your time is minimal, then simply study the leading vloggers in your industry. Look for these vlogs on YouTube, and after that, select those with the greatest amount of members and video views. This is going to be time extremely well spent and ought to provide you with a great deal of excellent ideas.

## Determine and Understand Your Audience

What type of audience are you searching for? Will your vlog be for individuals who wish to take a trip to amazing locations throughout the world? Or find out how to earn money on the internet? Or discover how to look lovely utilizing budget plan makeup?

Discover as much about your audience as you are able to. What do they truly wish to know? What are the typical concerns which they have? What blog sites or vlogs do they go to now?

## What Vlog Brand Name Will You Utilize?

You require a name for your channel and vlog. You might utilize your personal name for this and plenty of individuals have actually achieved success doing this. Or you could select a particular name for your vlog, which shows what it refers to. Here are several instances. ( A few of these might, in fact, exist so examine first):

- Stunning You-- a makeup vlog.

- Unique Locations - a travel vlog.

- Online Earnings-- make money on the web vlog.

So it is time for you to get a tad imaginative. Plan ahead when you are conceptualizing vlog name ideas. With an effective vlog, you could develop and promote your own products, so an appealing name is going to definitely assist here.

**Why You Need To Release Your Vlog on YouTube**

Here are certain engaging reasons why you need to establish your vlog on YouTube:

- There are more than 1 billion people on YouTube.

- Each day YouTube receives 4 billion video views.

- You could be successful in any YouTube niche.

- Mobile phones represent 1 billion views each day.

Is that amazing enough for you? Look, individuals like to view videos on all sorts of various topics. They are going to utilize YouTube as an online search engine to discover what they desire. It is the second biggest online search engine on the planet after Google. In case your channel offers what those searchers are trying to find, then you are going to get views. You can then inform your visitors to go and check out your site (or Facebook page etc.) for more amazing things. Provide an excellent reward to join your e-mail list, and they are going to do it. Yes, there are other video websites like Vimeo and

Daily Motion. These websites get a respectable quantity of traffic; however, they are miles from YouTube. If anybody informs you that YouTube is saturated then simply disregard them. It is the only way for your vlog.

## Develop Channel Art and Your YouTube Channel

A YouTube channel with no channel art does not generate an excellent impression. So invest time creating and designing suitable channel art for your vlog. In case graphic design is not your thing, then head to Fiverr.com and locate somebody who is proficient at it. Tell them what your channel is going to be about and provide your ideas for the channel art style. It is going to just cost you a couple of dollars to have fantastic channel art developed. This is well worth it. You are going to additionally require a little image for your channel symbol. This is your vlog logo.

When you have actually decided on this, you are able to include it into all of your videos and on your promoting moving forward. If you do not currently have a YouTube account, then you are going to want to make a cost-free Google account at https://www.google.com/. This is really simple to do and is going to require you less than 5 minutes. With your Google account established to go to YouTube.com and log in with your Google account. Then head to https://www.youtube.com/create_channel and make your vlog channel utilizing your brand name. After establishing your channel, I strongly advise that you develop a custom-made URL for your channel. To accomplish this, your YouTube account has to be more than one month old and you are going to require approximately 100 channel subscribers. You are going to additionally require an image of yourself and channel art. As soon as you are at this point, head to https://support.google.com/youtube/answer/26579 68?hl=en for accurate directions on how to develop your custom-made channel URL. This is truly worth doing.

## Plan the Content You Are Going To Develop

Okay, so your channel is good to go and the following action is to post some videos. Have a look at other effective vlogs for motivation here. How did they begin? Consider including aspects to your videos that you are going to feature constantly. For some, this is going to be a peek at the comments. For other folks, this is a recap.

If individuals enjoy these identifiable portions, they are going to return for more and are highly likely to subscribe. Plan the initial couple of weeks of video development, and after that, set up these. Dedicating these to a schedule is going to assist to inspire you. Keep in mind that consistency is the trick to a prosperous vlog.

# Chapter 4: Producing Great Videos

It is simply sound judgment that you wish to develop the most appealing, inspiring and helpful videos that you can. Eventually, after a certain amount of time devoted to producing videos for your vlog, you might well discover that you can develop excellent videos on the fly. Until you reach that stage, I suggest that you follow the actions listed beneath.

## Develop a Script

The majority of folks simply can't sit in front of a video camera and talk easily about their topic. In the event that you can, then terrific-- if not, then the ideal thing to do is to produce a script. Consider what you wish for every video to accomplish when preparing your script. Do you want the audience to act after viewing? The most vital parts of a video are the start and completion. Make the beginning actually engaging to inspire the audience to view all the way through. Remember that many folks have extremely short attention spans, and in case you do not make a great start with your videos, then even enthusiastic fans are not going to view the video.

You want to make the conclusion of the video really motivating too. This is specifically essential if you wish for them to take a particular action, such as checking out your site. In case you have no particular call to action in your mind, then provide a flavor of what the following video is going to be about. Make certain that your video script flows smoothly. In case you will demonstrate to your audience how to perform something then plan what you want to carry out and when. In case you are filming outdoors, then where are you going to go initially, secondly, and so on? After preparing your script, develop a storyboard. In case you are planning to narrate over the top of the video, then practice this. Keep in mind to maintain your videos as brief as you are able to. In case a tutorial will be lengthy, split it up into 2 or 3 videos.

## What About Tools?

OK, I did state at the beginning of this manual that you might make a video for your vlog with simply your mobile phone. You could start in this manner; however, there are far better methods to create your videos. This all begins with a high-quality camcorder.

You do not require an expert digital camera to film your vlog videos. Whenever your vlog achieves success and you are bringing in income, then go and obtain a professional camera. Until then, simply utilize a high-quality camcorder which is going to film in HD. In case you will shoot videos inside, then you want to consider lighting. Record some test video footage to see how desirable the lighting is. Buy some lights in case you have to. It is useless investing in a top-quality video camera if the lighting is bad. You require a high-quality mic too. In case you develop videos with bad audio quality, then you are certainly not going to prosper with your vlog. For interior recording, acquire a premium USB microphone.

What about screen recording and video modifying? In case you are planning to produce tutorials, then you might wish to film your computer system screen. Desktop recording is simple with Camtasia; however, this is going to be priced at around $200. There is a cost-free alternative which is CamStudio. Give this a shot initially. CamStudio is going to just work on Windows-based computer systems. In case you have a Mac, then you can have a go at macOS Mojave. There are additional cost-free screen recording apps for Macs. After recording your video, you are going to want to edit it to render it the very best it could be. If you have Camtasia or CamStudio at that point, both of these are going to do an excellent job. There are cost-free video editing apps accessible for Mac and Windows users. Windows Movie Maker is an excellent video editing set for Windows users, and in case you own a Mac, then utilize iMovie. You are going to find both of these apps user-friendly and you can include shifts and other functions to produce your videos appear truly fantastic.

**Developing Your Video**

Talk with enthusiasm in your voice. Do not be dull and boring. This is going to drive individuals away quicker than you could envision. Be passionate during the video. You simply cannot expect your viewers to be passionate about your videos if you are not. If you are developing a tutorial, then offer evidence that your approaches truly work. If other individuals utilize your approaches, then ask them to supply a video review. Include as much social proof as you are able to. Appeal to individuals' feelings as much as feasible within your video. Tell them how interesting it is going to be for them to take a trip to the location you are shooting in. Or tell them how gorgeous they are going to look after utilizing your make up ideas.

## Test How Well Your Videos are Received.

In your head, you have actually developed an excellent video; however, what truly counts is what your audience believes. You want to take a look at a couple of things here, like the number of viewers who saw your video from start to finish? If that wasn't the case for a great deal of viewers, at what phase of the video did they quit viewing it? Is there an issue with a particular part of the video? How many individuals liked the video, and how many provided it with a "thumbs down"?

Check out the remarks and see if there are any critiques there. Do not take them individually. Treat them as great feedback to produce greater videos down the road. What can you do in case your video was not effectively received? Well, you may either edit it to include the information that individuals in the comments state was lacking, or you can produce a brand-new video which deals with this. So now you understand how to develop excellent videos which are going to keep individuals engaged and desiring more from your vlog. Choose the majority circulation. With all videos, you can always count on people who have a grievance. In case most of the viewers love your video, then you are on the correct track.

Constantly ask viewers of your videos to sign up for your channel in case they have not. Ask them to "like" the video too and motivate them to leave comments to ensure that you could produce greater videos in the future. Inform your audience that your vlog is for them, so any feedback is really useful. Do whatever you are able to to appeal to individuals' feelings. Tell them that they can accomplish whatever you are demonstrating to them. Utilize words like "amazing," "great" and other superlatives. And constantly be enthusiastic in your videos!

# Chapter 5: Optimizing Your Youtube Videos

Optimizing your videos correctly is vital. When you are first beginning, this is truly crucial as you want to do whatever that you can to guarantee that your videos show up in a YouTube search. It is going to additionally increase your odds of your videos ranking higher in Google too.

## All of it Begins With Keyword Research

You want to learn what individuals are most likely to type into the search box on YouTube to discover your videos. The ideal method to accomplish this is through keyword research. You might do this completely free, utilizing the Google Keyword Planner. You will need to make a cost-free Google Adwords account to gain access to this tool. Let's state that you are developing a video about taking a trip to Japan. When you are in the Google Keyword Planner type in the seed keyword "Japan Travel" and after that, see what other keyword recommendations Google has to provide. You can download these ideas in a CSV file which you can open with the majority of spreadsheet applications like Microsoft Excel. Look at the list and pick the ideal keywords. Take a look at the approximated search volumes. You wish to create a list of around 10 keywords for every video. Choose which keyword is going to be your "primary" keyword. Perhaps this could be "travel to Japan."

## Produce a Compelling Headline Around Your Primary Keyword

You want to come up with an attractive headline so that when individuals see your video in the search results page, they will wish to see it. So for our Japan instance, you might utilize something like "Travel To Japan For Fun And Enjoyment." Make certain that you include your primary keyword in the title. Do not simply leave the title as "Travel To Japan." This will not influence that many folks to view your video. Utilize other words to produce enthusiasm. Another method might be "Travel To Japan-- You Will Not Believe What Happened!" This produces interest. Attempt composing a variety of various titles with your keyword in them. Choose 10 various titles, and after that, pick the very best one. In case you can get the keyword in at the start of the title, at that point, this is more suitable, yet it doesn't matter that much. So simply go crazy here with your ideas. Keep in mind that the more alluring you make your title, the more views you are going to get.

## Compose a Keyword-Rich Description

Some individuals like to check out the description of a video before they see it, so make this engaging also. I suggest that your description is at the very least 300 words long and includes the secondary keywords that you discovered previously. Inform individuals what the video refers to, however, do not provide everything. You can constantly state something like, "you will not believe what happened by the end of this video" or "I have a huge surprise for you by the end of the video." Simply utilize tactics to hook the audience and motivate them to see all the way through. Do not go nuts with keywords in the description. In case you can't fit them in organically, do not include them.

## Utilize the Appropriate Tags for Your Video

Just utilize keywords in tags that relate to your video. If your video has to do with traveling to Japan, then do not include unassociated keywords in like "how to speak Chinese." If somebody is aiming to understand Chinese and sees your video, they are going to be really unimpressed that there is very little about learning Chinese within it. So pick about 5 associated keywords (involving your primary keyword) and include these as tags. There is a 400 character limitation on tags with YouTube at the moment of composing. This does not indicate that you need to utilize every last character.

## Make Sure to Articulate your Primary Keywords in the Video

This one may amaze you. The important thing is that technology has actually truly advanced over the last couple of years, and YouTube can comprehend English (and perhaps other languages), so it will detect particular essential expressions. No one understands simply how precise the YouTube system is for acknowledging spoken keywords; however, estimates propose as high as 80%. This is going to continuously improve, so it is truly worth stating your primary keyword and certain secondary keywords within your video. Make sure to prepare for this when producing your video script.

## Excellent Video Optimization Does Not Take Long

If you have actually devoted a lot of time producing a storyboard and a video script as I recommended, then it appears insane not to devote a couple of minutes optimizing your videos to ensure that they have the optimum possibility of being discovered in a search. So utilize these video optimization pointers each time. Do not avoid the keyword research phase, as this is the most crucial activity. It is not going to require you long to reveal some excellent keywords. Even if you have a big following with your vlog, I would regularly advise that you optimize every video.

# Chapter 6: Promoting Your Vlog

When you produce your brand-new vlog and begin to post your videos, you need to do more than simply depend on the optimization strategies we went over in the last chapter for search traffic. You want to inform the world about your fresh vlog! It is never ever an instance of "create it and they are going to come." You want to put in some constant advertising effort to offer your vlog every opportunity of establishing a big following. Certain vloggers wait up until they have a variety of videos on their vlog like 10 to 30, yet my suggestion is to begin promoting your blog site immediately after your initial video is up. If you do not have a substantial social media following, then do not allow that to stop you. Some vloggers started with social profiles of less than 50 fans and now they are doing extremely well. The crucial thing is to be consistent.

## Inform Everybody That You Know

Make a list of all of your members of the family, buddies, work coworkers previous and present and any other individuals who you know. Utilize Facebook, e-mail and any other methods that you have to call them and tell them about your brand-new vlog. In case you have not talked to a few of these individuals in years, write them a pleasant e-mail and let them know that you miss them. Ask them to connect with you once again in case you wish to do that. After that, tell them that you have actually begun a brand-new vlog and that you would truly value their help. This is something which is so simple to do; however, the majority of folks do not perform it. Unless you have a great reason for not telling individuals you currently know about your vlog, then let them know! It could be a great deal of fun reaching out to individuals you have actually not contacted in a while. Ask them to get the word out to the folks who they know as well.

## Utilize Reddit

In case you do not have a Reddit account, then register for one today. It is an incredibly popular network that is neglected by the majority of people. Individuals make Sub Reddits that are devoted to particular topics and specific niches. Not all of these are going to be a winner for you. Nevertheless, here are some excellent ones for fresh vloggers:

-/ r/NewTubers.

-/ r/vlog.

-/ r/vlogs.

-/ r/vlogger.

-/ r/vlogging.

As soon as you get your Reddit account, utilize it to talk about other individuals' accounts. Attempt to develop an account which fits your vlog brand. Make sure to follow the guidelines on Reddit as you can get your account closed extremely rapidly if they believe you are spamming. Have a look at what others carry out in the Sub Reddits pointed out above.

**Use Facebook**

You can not and should not neglect the largest social media network. Facebook is a fantastic location for publishing videos and getting individuals to share your material. Produce a Facebook Page around your vlog brand name. It is truly simple to do and there are a lot of YouTube videos to demonstrate to you how to accomplish this successfully. Include branded artwork on your Facebook page. Make it appear truly expert. Make sure to publish other helpful material on your page along with your vlog videos. End up being friends with other individuals on Facebook that remain in your niche. Search For Facebook Groups which you could sign up with that are related as well. Facebook has an excellent marketing service where you can precisely target your audience to push traffic to your Facebook Page. It is not merely about obtaining "likes" for your page. Motivate individuals to leave comments and share too.

**Use Twitter**

Twitter is a big social media network that it could be tough to have success with. However, it deserves the effort due to the fact that with a big Twitter following, you could truly increase subscriptions to your vlog. Once again, do not simply create tweets about your vlogs. In case this is all that you do, then individuals are going to stop reacting to your tweets. Post some other beneficial tweets and re-tweet material from various other Twitter users that relates to your vlog. Prospering with Twitter (just like with other social networks) is all about connecting with others. Follow individuals who you think have an interest in your industry and respond to the tweets that they create and retweet them. Share their material as much as you manage.

## Use Instagram

A great deal of individuals avoid Instagram since it could be challenging to get a following there. However, it is truly worth persisting with it as you are able to get a great deal of YouTube views from this network. Instagram users like photos, along with videos. So take a fascinating screenshot from your vlogs and publish this asking individuals to take a look. Something you want to understand about Instagram is that you can't link straight to your YouTube vlog from posts. They do not enable external links. So you want to establish a great bio on Instagram and link to your vlog from there. When you create a post, inform individuals that the link to your vlog remains in your bio. It is constantly an excellent idea to inform individuals precisely what you wish for them to do.

## Use Quora

Quora.com is an online forum where questions are posed on almost each subject imaginable. It has a substantial user base and is typically neglected as a marketing tool for vloggers. It is likewise a fantastic location to get motivation for potential videos for your vlog. Discover concerns which have a direct connection to videos on your vlog. Compose a response, and after that, include something such as "for a more comprehensive response to this, please have a look at this video." In case your video does a truly excellent job addressing the concern, it is going to get a great deal of "upvotes," which indicates that a growing number of Quora users are going to see it.

## Make Comments on Videos Published by Prominent YouTubers

While it holds true that there are a great deal of idiots who make foolish comments on a lot of YouTube videos (you are going to need to handle this on your own at some phase), there are actually a great deal of real individuals who leave comments too. Your task is to turn into one of these authentic individuals who leave practical comments. Discover other associated videos in your niche and leave a favorable comment about it. By entering into the discussion and adding value to other individuals' videos, there is a likelihood that they are going to reciprocate by clicking your username and taking a look at your channel. This is among the most convenient and most reliable methods to get more subscribers and views, so make certain that you perform this. It is really essential that you select the videos of prominent YouTubers who have some relation to your vlog. You do not need to simply include positive comments to popular videos either. Discover other associated top-quality videos which do not have as many views and add comments to those as well. Do not utilize a spam technique here-- never ever ask the video poster to take a look at your channel and subscribe.

## Utilize the YTTalk Online Forum

Sign up with the YTTalk online forum. It is an extremely active online forum for the YouTube community, and there are individuals there with little and big channels. Begin adding to other individuals' posts and after that, utilize the online forum as a feedback system for your videos.

Individuals who publish videos on YouTube have a tendency to view other individuals' videos too, so this is an excellent place to discover additional subscribers and viewers. As always, seek to bring in value with your posts and responses. Do not turn to any kind of spam.

## Use Empire.Kred

Many vlog owners have actually never ever even heard of Empire.Kred. When you register, you are granted a stock value based upon your social impact. You can publish your vlog material here and convince other influencers on the platform to take a look and engage with it. Other influencers on Empire.Kred could acquire stock in you in case they enjoy what you are doing. This is going to boost the quantity of "eaves" that you possess (the digital currency utilized). You could utilize your eaves to develop particular tasks like asking for other influencers to see your newest video and so on. You are not permitted to request particular engagement activities like sharing, commenting or liking. Simply leave it to the influencer to generate their own choices on this. Influencers are going to gain eaves from you for finishing the job. In case the influencers enjoy your vlog, they are going to register for your channel.

## Engage With All Comments You Get

The ideal method to promote your vlog is to develop a community. As you expand your community, increasingly more individuals are going to return to your videos and share them, leave comments and like them. You want to keep an eye on comments on all of your videos and react to them as quickly as you are able to. Individuals are going to actually value that you put in the time to react to their comments. You are showing that you are a genuine individual and appreciate what they have to state. This is going to inspire them to subscribe in case they have not currently done so and watch out for your potential videos.

# Chapter 7: Free Tools for Growing Your Youtube Channel

There are certain necessary resources which you could utilize to expand your YouTube channel, and the bright side is that they are all free of charge. The majority of them are simple to utilize and the advantages are quite apparent. Let's have a look at a few of the most effective cost-free tools.

## TubeBuddy

The significant advantage of utilizing TubeBuddy is that it is going to conserve you a great deal of time. It likewise supplies you with some excellent guidelines to truly grow your YouTube channel. TubeBuddy is an internet browser app that works with the most frequently utilized internet browsers like Mozilla Firefox, Google Chrome, and Safari. When you utilize TubeBuddy, you are going to discover that it has lots of beneficial functions from examining the SEO of your videos to assisting you with promoting your channel. There are thorough training videos offered that discuss everything truly well. You could actually conserve hours every week with this app. You could do a lot with the cost-free variation of TubeBuddy, and I recommend that you begin with this. If you desire more functions, then there is a Pro plan offered for $9 a month, a Star bundle for $19 a month, and a Legend plan for $49 a month.

## YouTube Creator Studio

This is one more cost-free app that is excellent for examining the efficiency of your channel and videos on the go. You can't really handle your videos with this app; however, you could do anything else. It is fantastic for discovering simply how well your videos are doing, as well as taking a look at the general functionality of your channel no matter where you are. There is a filter function where you could react to comments and develop that necessary connection with your audience. This function alone makes the app worth setting up on your mobile phone.

## Buffer.com

I described to you in the prior chapter that utilizing social networks to grow your YouTube channel and vlog is extremely advised. To assist you in sharing your videos on social media networks, the Buffer app is a truly fantastic resource. With Buffer, you could arrange and publish your material on Facebook, Instagram, Twitter, LinkedIn and Pinterest. There is one easy control panel for handling every little thing. The cost-free Buffer plan is for no more than 3 social profiles, and you can arrange 10 posts a month as a single user. In case you possess more than 3 social profiles or plan to create more than 10 posts a month, then there are premium plans you may opt for beginning at $15 a month. Whichever plan you select, you are going to conserve a great deal of time in case you utilize Buffer to arrange your posts. There is a web browser extension which you could utilize to publish content instantly to Facebook, Pinterest and Twitter.

## Audio Hero

It might be a genuine difficulty to discover terrific royalty-free music for your YouTube videos. Audio Hero makes discovering excellent music and sound effects for your videos truly simple. There is a substantial library of more than 250,000 music clips and sound effects to pick from, so you ought to never ever have any trouble discovering what you desire. Even though the Audio Hero app is free of charge, to utilize the soundtracks, you are going to need to pay a little fee. This is a lot more desirable than running the risk of encroaching on copyright and even having your videos eradicated. During the time of composing, you can acquire 50 downloads of royalty-free music clips for just $9.99.

## Snappa

Developing your personal graphics or discovering a great and dependable graphic designer might be a genuine headache. You understand that you require top quality graphics to expand your YouTube channel, so what do you do? Simply utilize Snappa, obviously! There are a great deal of premade design templates you can utilize in Snappa. You could utilize Snappa quickly to produce your preliminary channel art for truly appealing video thumbnails as you publish your videos. It is actually crucial that your thumbnails look terrific. This could actually be the distinction between someone viewing your video and another person's. The cost-free variation has 5,000 design templates and you are able to develop 5 graphics a month. In case you desire more, then plans begin at $10 a month.

## Repost for Instagram

Repost for Instagram is one more beneficial app for your Android or iPhone phone. You really should take Instagram into consideration as an excellent social platform to promote your vlog. It has a big user base which is growing constantly. When you have the Repost for Instagram app, you are going to have the ability to repost images or videos that your fans shared. You could incorporate the username of the individual that shared the material so that they get the credit, and your fans can quickly check them out.

# Chapter 8: Methods to Monetize Your Vlog

OKAY, so you have your YouTube channel established properly, you have actually published some vlog videos and you are striving to boost your subscriber amount and video views. Where is the benefit in all of this? This manual has to do with vlogging for income, so I will show you a few of the very best methods to generate income from your vlog here. The reality is that there are various manners in which you could generate income from your videos and vlog.

## YouTube Partner

When you end up being a YouTube Partner, you are able to show Google Adsense advertisements on videos that you pick. If you are not familiar with Google Adsense, it is utilized by publishers (like vloggers and blog site owners) to show Google Advertisements in or on their content. Each time an advertisement is clicked you share the income with YouTube. Now the initial thing to state here is that it is not likely that you are going to make life-altering earnings with Google Adsense on your videos even if you have countless views. There are likewise numerous aspects which impact just how much of the income you get like:

- The amount of views an advertisement gets (not all viewers of your video are going to discover the advertisement).

- The duration of time that the advertisement was visible (some advertisements are really brief videos).

- Was there any engagement with the advertisement?

- The demographics of your target market.

- The number of marketers that wish to promote in your niche at the existing time.

As you have actually most likely figured out, it is hard to forecast the cash you are going to make by making it possible for Google Adsense on your videos. However, you do not need to stress over any of the aspects above, aside from attempting to get as many views to your video as achievable. There are various kinds of Google Adsense advertisements that you can show on your videos. Among the most typical is a basic banner showing at the base of the video. There are likewise brief video trailers which could be shown at the beginning, throughout your video or at the conclusion. In some cases, the audience is able to skip these trailers and on other occasions, they are going to need to view them.

You are going to have to fulfill a variety of requirements to be qualified for the YouTube Partner Program and showing Google Adsense advertisements. The guidelines alter typically, so it is ideal to go to https://support.google.com/youtube/answer/72851#eligibility to see what the most recent guidelines are. As soon as you are a verified partner, it is simple to generate income from any of your videos by logging into your YouTube profile and making it possible for monetization. There are a variety of payment approaches which you could select from consisting of a check, electronic funds transfer, wire transfer, Western Union and more. You want to think thoroughly about making it possible for these advertisements on your videos. Some audiences are not going to mind an Adsense banner at the base of the video. A trailer at the beginning which can not be skipped might try out the patience of several visitors though, particularly in case they are brand-new to your vlog.

## Affiliate Marketing

With affiliate marketing, you advertise other individuals' items and when a sale is made, you make a commission. Commissions vary from extremely little (a couple of cents) to huge (hundreds of dollars) for high ticket products. Videos are a great deal more convincing than composed text, so you might be showing an item or a piece of software application while including your affiliate link within the description. Certain individuals who own makeup vlogs for instance succeed on a monthly basis via affiliate marketing. With a lot of vlog specific niches, there are going to be affiliate services and products which you could advertise. You simply want to discover them. Utilize Google or another online search engine and enter the kind of service or a product, and after that, "affiliate program." So an instance would be "cosmetics affiliate program." You can advertise physical items and digital items too. Digital items would generally be software applications, a "how-to" guide, instruction videos, and so forth. It could be more difficult to make a sale with digital items, yet the commissions are typically a great deal higher than with tangible goods.

## Merchandising

You could develop your personal merchandising for your vlog brand. A fine instance of this is a t-shirt or sweatshirt with your brand name logo on it or perhaps caps. There are businesses you could utilize that are going to provide the clothing or caps in the appropriate sizes and colors with your design engraved on them. There are other merchandising items which are rather simpler than clothing like USB memory sticks with your logo design, calendars with your logo, pens with your logo design, phone cases, and a lot more. It is simple to discover a business which is going to brand prominent products for you. Merchandising is not a thing which you have to consider when you are initially beginning with your vlog. You are going to require a great deal of active subscribers to earn a profit from merchandising. Once you attain that big subscriber foundation, then you can offer a great deal of merchandise products and bring in good cash.

## Offering Your Own Products/Services

This is something which you may do relatively rapidly with your vlog. There are various services and products that you are able to offer from your vlog. Here are certain instances:

- A book.

- A "how-to" tutorial.

- A video training course.

- Training services.

The ideal method to accomplish this is to instruct your audience about the essentials of accomplishing something, and after that, inform them that they require your product in case they would like to know the advanced techniques. Offer value within your videos to get your audience hooked, however, do not deliver everything free of charge. Among the most ideal methods to offer your services and products is via e-mail marketing. You could utilize an e-mail autoresponder service like Aweber or get a response and offer something of value free of charge as a reward for joining your e-mail list. You are going to want to do this from your site or blog site and after that include this link in your video description. Inform individuals in your videos of the advantages of joining your e-mail list. Tell them that you are going to supply them with more cost-free ideas and recommendations, but just if they register for your list.

## Brand Sponsorship

In case you can get a brand name sponsorship offer, then you do not need to stress over showing advertisements or offering anything. You are going to get payment from the sponsor due to the fact that they want you to advertise what they provide on your vlog. It is immediately related to your vlog and is going to assist your audience. You are going to want to touch on your sponsor in the videos. The majority of the time, sponsors discover vloggers. They will just wish to deal with vloggers who have a big subscriber base, so this could require some time to occur. In case you have a great deal of subscribers and your videos have big view counts, at that point, the sponsors are going to call you.

## Financing Platforms

There are now funding platforms like Patreon.com which make it possible for vlog fans to establish a month to month membership to finance their preferred vloggers and keep them going. A great deal of vloggers are now relying on platforms such as Patreon for a routine month-to-month earnings. With Patreon, you can set different levels of memberships. You are going to want to provide your Patreon subscribers with something more than what your regular vlog subscribers get. They want to feel unique and pleased that they are financing you monthly.

## Chapter 9: Vlogging Best Practices

In case you want your vlog to be effective, there are a couple of best practices that I strongly suggest that you embrace. These best practices are followed by all effective vloggers, so you want to pay very close attention here and comply with them too.

## Constantly Produce Top Quality Videos

Constantly put your audience first. What are they searching for? Which responses do they require to resolve issues in their life? How can you make their life more interesting and how could you captivate your audience? Never ever submit low-grade videos to your vlog since you feel under pressure to provide your audience with something. It is constantly about quality and not quantity. If you produce something of poor quality, then you are going to lose your audience. Simply do not do this! Utilize excellent tools and software applications to develop your videos. You do not need the most pricey digital camera on the marketplace, however, you do have to produce videos which are clear with great sound quality. Never ever utilize a poor-quality mic. Constantly be enthusiastic and delighted in your videos. In case you are not enthusiastic, how could you expect your viewers to be?

## Consistency

When you begin pumping out your top quality videos, then your audience is going to yearn for increasingly more from you. You want to be consistent and produce videos to a schedule of some type. If you leave it too long between one video and the following, you are going to lose individuals. You want to be persistent with your vlog. OK, several vlogs have actually taken off truly rapidly and made their owners a great deal of cash in record time. However, this is the exception instead of the rule. Take your time and be persistent and concentrate on being dependable with quality and publishing schedules.

## Concentrate on Getting More Subscribers

Do not concentrate on cash; concentrate on getting brand-new subscribers. Do whatever you are able to to get the word out about your vlog. When the subscribers arrive, so will the cash. Utilize social networks thoroughly and attempt other approaches to promote your vlog.

## Know What is Working

YouTube has a great deal of analytics to assist you in figuring out what your videos are doing the best. So, utilize this to find what is working and what is not. Do more of what is working! Fine-tune things to make them much better. Examine your videos for the right optimization approach.

## Conclusion of Vlogging

There has never ever been a greater time to begin a vlog, and I have offered you all that you require within this book to plan and execute effectively. The need for premium vlogs is going to keep on increasing so enter now to use the increasing trend. Videos will constantly be the favored medium for Web users. Individuals slouch and if they can devote 5 minutes to see a video on how to perform something, this is a lot simpler than investing 20 minutes going through a 5,000-word article. With a vlog, you have a terrific chance to engage with your audience.

Ask them questions within your videos and ask that they leave you responses in the comments area. You could, after that, thank them by responding to their comments. You want to do every little thing which you could to expand your vlog. This is going to boost your capacity to generate income from it. So make certain to optimize all of your videos correctly and keep getting the word out on social networks. So now it is over to you. Begin arranging your brand-new vlog today. If you have to purchase some top quality recording tools, then do so. It is going to definitely be worth it, and it will reinforce your dedication to your vlog. I wish you excellence with your vlog!

# Viral Marketing

Guide to Successfully Creating a Buzz Around
Your Online Brand, Acquiring Social Media
Audience and Bringing in the Profits

By Adam Torbert

# Introduction to Viral Marketing

Let's get one thing crystal clear: a lot of folks attempt "viral marketing" and fall short. The reason ought to be apparent. The majority of folks have no idea what viral marketing is truly all about. As a matter of fact, the more they hear the phrase, the more bewildered they become. This raises the chance that they are going to burn and crash whenever they attempt "viral marketing."

Allow me to clue you in on a secret. The key to viral marketing is all about entering into a niche network of individuals.

Believe it or not, folks intrigued by whatever it is you are advertising are already gathering online. Perhaps they follow a particular prominent Twitter profile. Perhaps they have joined a wide variety of Facebook pages and groups. A lot of these are devoted to this audience.

The majority of folks who attempt viral marketing are unaware of this. They don't even understand that this niche network currently exists.

So what is the trick? It's as easy as entering the appropriate network and 'resharing' content which has previously gone viral. There it is. The cat is out of the bag.

Lots of folks fall short with this kind of marketing since they believe that they need to come up with their own stuff. What they're truly striving to accomplish is reinvent the wheel. Why must you roll the dice with content which has a substantial likelihood of not heading anywhere? Concentrate instead on something that's currently well-known with your audience members.

You, after that, take something that's in demand on Twitter and reshare it on Facebook in addition to on many other Twitter accounts which might not have discovered the viral content you're sharing. Leverage various sharing platforms' tagging systems and additional audience recognition methods.

YouTube, Twitter, Facebook and other social media networks want you to be successful. They wish for your content to proliferate. Why? The more prominent your content ends up being, the more traffic they receive.

It's in their benefit for you to have the instruments you require to market your content. The more noticeable you end up being, the higher the possibility you're going to attract new folks to their platforms. This is the reason why all these networks have their personal tagging and visibility-enhancing systems. Utilize those systems. Acquire traffic from them. Lead all this traffic back to your landing page.

In which way are you planning to convert individuals? Well, you might try demonstrating an ad to them. When you put the appropriate ad before the appropriate eyeballs, you might receive a great deal of clicks. A few of those clicks might transform into hard, cold dollars.

Preferably, you ought to transform as much of your traffic into mailing list members as you can. You can additionally get them to take a look at your blog, and in case they enjoy what they read, register to your mailing list. As soon as you have a great deal of folks on your mailing list and they are really dedicated to your content, odds are, you could transform that mailing list into a recurring income source.

This book reveals the tricks to viral marketing which enables you to save time, save cash, and stay clear of unneeded stress. It goes without saying, if you follow the suggestions which I will share in this book, you boost your odds of finally thriving with viral marketing.

# Chapter 1: You Don't Have to Just Another Viral Marketing Failure

## Don't Join the Legion of Viral Content Failures

The substance of viral marketing is content. Simply put, you need to obtain viral content so you could draw in a great deal of traffic from various spots on the web and convert that traffic into money.

The issue is, it's too simple to fall short producing "viral" content. It truly is.

A lot of marketers have an attitude that in case they "create it, they are going to come." I'm sorry, but releasing "hot, incredible or imaginative content" on your website is not going to cut it. Posting excellent content is insufficient to make it go viral.

It's quite costly to produce original content. You most likely already understand that first hand. Perhaps you attempted hiring somebody to compose this content for you. Perhaps you attempted creating it yourself.

Despite how you attempted to accomplish it, the lesson is still identical. It's pricey. Either you pay in the form of cash or you pay in the form of time.

**Viral Success All Comes Down To the Correct Eyeballs**

Simply put, you want to get niche visitors. The trick to viral marketing is not enormous amounts of views. It is not an immensely mind-boggling volume of traffic. Believe it or not, organic views or organic visibility will not equate to much cash. Really.

Millions of views won't create true money, unless those views are from the correct eyeballs. Unless you're simply attempting to earn money off YouTube videos and you earn money per thousand views, traffic, per se, won't pay the bills.

## Viral Content Pieces are Not Commodities

I understand I've said to you that one vital aspect to successful viral marketing is to discover things that have obtained traction on Facebook and reshare it on Twitter in addition to YouTube. However, there is a limit.

Please recognize that even if it's trendy on Twitter, it doesn't automatically indicate it is going to achieve the identical traction on Pinterest, Facebook or Instagram. Besides, in case you're sharing video, it's tough to accomplish that on Pinterest. Pinterest is tailored just to pictures.

While you might get a fair bit of traffic, please recognize that it's not as easy as simply moving content from one network to another.

## Viral Popularity Doesn't Matter

I know you're most likely surprised. You're most likely thinking, "Are you nuts? Do you want to tell me that if my content receives a ton of likes, comments and favorites, my stuff is still lousy?" Yes, that's effectively what I'm attempting to say.

Those measurements don't make a difference. Do you know what makes a difference? Retweets or shares. Those are the only user activities that make a difference since they have a direct role in identifying how much and how frequently your material gets redistributed everywhere.

It doesn't truly matter if you possess a piece of content which gets a great deal of commentary and has a bunch of likes and favorites. That won't aid you. You require the correct eyeballs.

Taking into consideration the reality that folks who follow other people or who have buddies have a tendency to have the identical shared interests, at that point it makes a bunch of sense to get your material shared as much as feasible. Whenever people share your stuff on Facebook, odds are, they are going to share it with folks who share the identical interest in your market. That's what you ought to be aiming for.

I've uncovered a bunch of secrets within this chapter. Please recognize that it's not about the content. Rather, it's about the correct eyeballs. You can't address viral content like some kind of commodity. Also, the large majority of social indicators don't truly matter when it pertains to viral marketing.

## Chapter 2: You can Find Viral Content Everywhere

### Viral Content Really is Everywhere!

Believe it or not, there are heaps of things going viral on Twitter and Facebook each and every day. Actually, based upon a relatively recent estimation, over 2 million new bits of content get posted each day. You best believe that a considerable amount of that goes viral on social networks and on the web generally.

Content goes viral constantly. There are a bunch of reasons for this. First, the content has some kind of emotional impact. Perhaps it's funny, perhaps it's stunning, perhaps it angers folks. No matter what the case might be, folks get so stirred up that they can't help but share that bit of content.

One more factor is just pure cuteness. If you continue discovering videos of adorable kittens, this is the adorable factor at play. This is quite self-explanatory. This could apply to babies, animals, or older folks doing entertaining stuff. Provided that something is doing something adorable, you could wager that there's a substantial chance that piece of content is going to get shared a ton.

One more popular reason for virality is the surprise factor. Folks are simply surprised or stunned by what's taking place in the video. Perhaps it involves some kind of crime. Maybe it includes something outrageous, disgraceful or scandalous.

Folks love to view something new. People enjoy getting thrown off every now and then. It's sort of like describing the allure of a train wreck. You understand you shouldn't watch those, however, folks do it regardless.

An additional explanation of why content goes viral is the pure surprise factor of newness. For instance, in case there is some kind of scientific revelation that truly blows people's minds, don't be shocked if it goes viral.

Lastly, the content may go viral if it mentions to you something which you don't currently know. Perhaps you actually know the content, but it resends the material in a really intriguing and appealing way. This kind of content is like some kind of brain treat.

These are the kinds of content which go viral each and every day. There's truly no particular niche preference. You might be viewing a viral video on a typically dull subject such as furniture, but there's something about the video which just captures your attention. You can't help but talk about it with your buddies.

## Psychological Foundation of Content Virality

Let's get something clear, whenever you're sharing stuff with your private network, you're putting yourself out there. It may detonate in your face. In case you share content which a bunch of folks find unacceptable, you might lose reputation. Still, folks share content on Twitter feeds and Facebook timelines constantly.

Why do they do this? What do they get from it? What are the psychological variables at play?

Well, firstly, people love to share content since they wish to be regarded as "hip." They wish to be seen as awesome or as folks who understand what's up with the web. They wish to be the first to share something exciting which is quickly ending up being viral on the web. There's an incredible emotional reward related to being the initial one to share intriguing material.

One more reason is merely to simply delight in and exercise one's own influence. I don't know about you, however, it makes me feel quite good when I share anything that I have an interest in or am enthusiastic about, and my buddies share and reshare those things.

Essentially, they validate me whenever I see that. They tell me, in numerous ways, that my viewpoint is significant. Every share that my material gets is a vote for my own authority, competence and trustworthiness.

Ultimately, folks share content since they just believe it is interesting or valuable. Simply put, it captures their range of individual interests.

And here is the key: if these people's systems are fine-tuned enough to the point that they essentially share the identical set of interests, you could guarantee that content is going to go viral.

Essentially, if you are fond of rabbits, and I love rabbits, and I upload videos of adorable rabbits, odds are, you are going to click the "share" button once you view my status update on your timeline. Odds are, you also have buddies who have an interest in the same things. You likely have buddies who have an interest in rabbits and they are going to share your content.

Never undervalue how "viral" shared interests might be since this is how Facebook is set up. Whenever you add people to your friend network, odds are, they're from a similar ambient as you. They have the identical experiences, you attended the identical school, and you might have a vast array of common interests. It is these overlapping common interests which give energy to virality.

## So What is the Honest truth Regarding Viral Content Marketing?

There are several points which you want to wrap your mind around. Accomplish this and you are going to flourish with viral marketing. Mess this up and you are going to keep on messing up long into the future. You are going to continue to have a hard time.

To begin with, you don't need to create something new. Next, you could recycle someone else's stuff. Lastly, you might reverse engineer your competitors' viral content and networks. Put this all together and you possess all that you require for a prosperous viral content marketing strategy.

## Chapter 3: Avoid This to Save Money and Time

Let's make one thing apparent, you certainly can attempt to come up with your personal content and expect that in some way it is going to become viral. You're more than invited to do so. But allow me to tell you, in case that is your plan, be ready to squander a great deal of money, time, and inspiration.

For me, there is not a thing more irritating than investing a great deal of time, work and emotional energy into anything and not observing any results: no traffic, no sales, no money. You only need to go through a couple of more days or weeks of that experience for you to wish to quit.

That is exactly why a bunch of folks fall short with viral marketing. They discover that it's not getting the job done, so they quit. The unfortunate truth is, they set themselves up to fall short. They dissapoint themselves.

How come? The aim for the incorrect strategy. They make an effort to come up with something hot, fresh, amazing, innovative, and groundbreaking. However, for each single marketer who can pull that off, there are numerous others who flop.

## My Recommendation to You is Not to Even Try

Let's get serious here. you think a content idea is in demand and " is going to go viral," it won't always indicate that it is going to. As a matter of fact, for the most part, that never occurs.

Unless you can read the minds of your target market members, you might be better off not creating your own material. Creating some new viral material can be costly both in terms of money and time.

## The Superior Way

So what is the ideal method to perform viral content marketing? To begin with, you have to focus on your niche. Keep in mind, not all the viral content on the market being shared repeatedly again are in your niche. As a matter of fact, the large majority are most likely not in your niche.

Focus rather on established winners in your particular niche. You have to check out the number of times they've been shared. You have to check out the number of times they have been retweeted. These are great signs of how truly viral they are.

It's incredibly important that you concentrate on how many shares a bit of content has received. This is a great sign of how "viral" it is.

Let me inform you, it doesn't make a difference how many people like it, comment on it, none of that makes a difference. Considering that when they perform that, they're not outright endorsing that bit of content to their ring of influence. They're not driving that bit of content to folks who might share the identical interests whenever they leave a comment or click the "like" button.

Don't fritter away time thinking about social engagement indicators that don't truly move the ball forward. Pay attention to what counts. Concentrate on how many times a bit of content has been shared or retweeted.

Once you have located this content and you ensured that it truly relates to your niche, incorporate a call to action to screen the eyeballs of niche audience members. This is a vital aspect of the procedure.

If you were simply going to poach niche material which has previously gone viral, you're not truly bringing in a lot of value. You're likewise creating pipe dreams for yourself.

How come? Well, odds are, the large majority of folks sharing that charming video which you discovered and reshared are not in your intended niche. You need to call people to action to a link coupled with that viral video or viral image which screens your niche audience members.

For instance, in case you are passing along a recording of a cat high fiving its owner, you might place a call to action saying, "For awesome cat training suggestions, check out this site."

Now, please recognize that the large majority of folks sharing that charming and funny video of a cat giving high fives most likely don't even have cats. They merely believe that the video is amusing. They just believe that it's adorable and remarkable. They think it places a smile on people's faces. But allow me to tell you, the majority of those folks are most likely not in your target market.

The bright side is, by placing a call to action with the material which you are 'resharing', certain folks who are members of your niche audience will click through. You have prequalified them. This is the way in which you piggyback on attempted and verified viral content which is either directly or to some degree pertaining to your target niche.

## Chapter 4: The Trick to Successful Viral Marketing

## The Trick to Effective Viral Marketing

I understand that I have pointed out this in the past chapter. However, to drive the point home, I will completely describe the crucial steps you need to make to carry out truly successful viral marketing campaigns. These viral marketing campaigns are going to do the job not just on your social networks but likewise on your website, your forum postings, and other internet marketing efforts.

## Step # 1: Find What's Hot

The initial thing which you want to accomplish is to find what's popular on the web. There are heaps of images, hyperlinks, image quotes, and videos going viral constantly. Folks can't aid but share this content.

## Identify Hot Stuff.

Now, soon after you have discovered this material, ensure that you screen them based upon how closely relevant they are to your intended niche. For instance, if you are advertising a plumbing service firm in Florida, you might share all the hilarious dogs riding scooters videos you desire. You may also get a great deal of traffic to your page. But guess what? You most likely will not schedule a lot of new appointments for your client utilizing these videos.

You could receive a great deal of eyeballs, but they are the incorrect ones. Why? The videos which you reshared and promoted are not relevant enough to your intended niche.

Niches are individuals who share particular issues. These are folks who are seeking particular common solutions. Be sure to have that in mind. Even if you get a bunch of traffic, it doesn't truly guarantee much.

## Step # 2: Share viral content to generate sales

It's truly important to recognize why you are carrying out viral marketing to begin with. This is where a bunch of folks flounder. They truly do. Why? They concentrate on raw numbers. They concentrate on acquiring as many clicks to their intended site as feasible.

Now, don't misunderstand me. Traffic is great, but it needs to be the correct kind of traffic.

If I had to pick between 1 million casual viewers or 1,000 highly targeted viewers, I would pick the latter each day. What's the point of acquiring 1 million viewers when just one in a million actually transforms into a paying client?

Compare that with acquiring 1,000 certified viewers and noticing 200, 300 or even 500 of them developing into actual paying customers. This is not rocket science. It ought to be rather apparent.

So recognize how this works and recognize what your attention ought to be on. It isn't about web traffic. It's something more. It's everything about driving sales.

You want to get the appropriate folks to the correct webpage so they might do anything which puts more cash in your bank account. That's the bottom line. That ought to be your objective.

This is why it's truly vital to share viral content to drive sales. You're not driving traffic, you're not attempting to optimize visibility, you're attempting to drive sales.

How do you accomplish this? Share the content on your blog. Reshare your blog's link on social networks. Utilize these to draw traffic to your website. You then transform this traffic into prospective sales by getting these prospects to register for your newsletter.

This is the way you play the game to triumph. You convert these prospects through a built-in blog page. The moment they click a link and they wind up on an engaging page of material, they might enjoy your content so much that they click on a link to get informed about your updates. That's the way you lock them in.

Or you provide a freebie like some kind of consumer manual. For instance, if your blog offers legal immigration services, you might wish to give away a free brochure which clues folks in on how to qualify to come to the USA on a tourist visa with very little inconveniences.

No matter what you do, get folks to register for your mailing list due to the fact that after they registered, you could then give them updates that could perhaps upsell them to affiliate items or get them to purchase your own goods. The possibilities are endless.

It is your email list which really does the difficult work of converting these folks. They may not read one update, however, if they check out an update and they like a link, you may transform that traffic into a possible sale. That's how effective a subscriber list is.

Your entire viral marketing strategy ought to be concentrated on driving conversions to your newsletter. The more folks are on your newsletter and the greater the quality of your updates, the more cash you can bring in eventually.

# Chapter 5: How to Locate the Right Content

## Finding Hot Content

Since you have an apparent idea of the two-step trick to successful viral marketing, how do you carry out step # 1? Well, there are two methods to accomplish it. You could take the difficult road or you could use the shortcut.

Just so you possess a transparent understanding of the manual screening process involved, I will explain these two choices thoroughly. First, you could attempt to perform things manually. You can get highly targeted material via this labor-intensive technique.

The initial thing which you have to accomplish is to head to Google Keyword Planner tool. In case you don't know what that is, register to Google Ads and click on their tools link, and you are going to be presented with a menu which provides the Google Keyword Planner resource.

Click on that tool. Input a couple of keywords directly pertaining to your niche. Keep accomplishing this and you are going to see lots of related keywords.

Once you obtain this substantial list, filter them based upon their precision or uniqueness to your niche. Once you have tidied up your keyword list, utilize these on Twitter or Facebook to look for social media accounts which focus on these keywords.

Naturally, you will just take into consideration social media accounts of individuals, companies or businesses who are really in your niche. You could tell by how they define themselves if they are in your intended niche.

Keep screening these accounts. At the conclusion of a lengthy process, you ought to have a lovely, clean list of social media accounts of your niche-particular rivals. These accounts could be on Instagram, Pinterest, Facebook, Twitter, YouTube, you name it. The lengthier your list, the better.

## Locate and Poach Your Competitors' or Niche Enthusiasts' Viral Content

Please keep in mind that whenever you actually click through the social media accounts of individuals and companies in your niche, you are going to promptly uncover that there really are two kinds of accounts: fans and competitors. I will not even define competitors due to the fact that this is self-explanatory.

Fan accounts are non-commercial accounts launched by folks who are simply emotionally committed to your niche. For instance, in case you are advertising dog training online programs, you could be able to obtain a big list of dog training social media accounts. The moment you check out their content, it's apparent that they're not truly doing this for cash. They're simply sharing their passions or excitement. These are fan accounts. You want to compile a substantial list of these too.

Once you have obtained a large list of niche-specific social media accounts, look at all their content. Check out at the number of times their content has been retweeted or reshared. Take note of photos, videos, intriguing links, picture quotes, or any other kind of media.

As you could perhaps tell, this procedure is not simple. You need to understand what you're doing. You need to understand what to search for. You likewise need to have plenty of time. Doing things laboriously could burn up plenty of time.

**The Faster Way: Buzzsumo.com**

In case you don't possess the patience or time to locate all your niche rivals' and niche fans' social media accounts and use their content, utilize BuzzSumo. This online resource is going to scour the primary social media networks for content which is directly pertaining to your niche keywords.

Ensure that you save the niche keywords which you received from Google Keyword Planner tool and utilize them at BuzzSumo. You are going to see a great deal of material which has been filtered readily based upon certain social indicators such as shares or retweets. BuzzSumo is a useful tool since it saves you a remarkable amount of time, work and frustration.

## Get Your Links All Set

When you have screened your competitors' most viral bits of content, take their URLs and place them in an Excel sheet. On the right side, look for the description for that bit of content. Typically, when you stumble upon viral content on a social media network, there's a brief description or even a headline. Make use of those materials.

## Chapter 6: How to Optimally Target Your Niche by Using the Right Content

## What is Curation?

When you have compiled your reverse-engineered content, please recognize that you will be utilizing them to create trustworthiness for your social media accounts and, eventually, to drive traffic to your intended website. Your target website might be material site, it might be a collection of article pages, or it might be an actual blog.

Regardless of how you set it up, you will be utilizing third-party material to establish a reputation for your accounts and create their following. What can draw traffic from those accounts to your target pages, websites or material sites or ads which you revolve in between curated material.

I hope this is apparent to you. You will be posting curated third party material on your social network account. Now, you might be asking, "Isn't this prohibited? Wouldn't these folks raise an objection?" No, they wouldn't.

It's a win/win scenario. You're driving traffic to them while simultaneously developing your own niche authority. You're likewise calling folks to action with their content to like your page, follow you on Instagram or Twitter or whichever other social media networks you're on.

You're establishing a win/win scenario. The folks behind the curated content receive traffic and brand exposure. You, meanwhile, get to develop your social media accounts.

As soon as you have a large following, an increasing amount of folks would then see the direct links to your sales pages. They are able to then click through and you wind up with additional traffic to your email squeeze page. This could result in a bigger email list, which could create a multitude of income opportunities in the future. That's how you play ball. It all comes down to reverse engineering and curating someone else's material.

## Improving Curated Content

I wish I could tell you that you are able to simply take third party viral material and promote them as is. This is exactly what a bunch of other marketers are doing. Sadly, in case you were to accomplish that, you will be leaving a bunch of cash on the table.

You need to comprehend that you're not simply attempting to inflate traffic with curated content. That should not be your primary objective. Your primary objective should not be traffic quantity. Rather, your primary objective is to get niche-targeted folks to see your content.

The more of these folks you reach out to, the more probable they are to click on the link to your social network account and end up being a follower or page liker or channel subscriber or fan. No matter what form it assumes, your goal is to obtain a large quantity of folks to follow you. You're attempting to establish a fan base.

And it will be tough to accomplish this in case you are simply sending out curated material with the same titles which were initially utilized. People could notice that your stuff is not truly original, so they likely would dismiss it. Besides, this stuff is viral so they've likely have viewed it prior from somewhere else.

Your initial step after you have screened curated content for niche uniqueness is to alter their headlines. Develop niche-targeted titles for all your curated content. Tighten the emphasis of this content.

For instance, in case you have a dropshipping shop which offers cat pendants and you have discovered really good viral videos of adorable kittens, ensure the title of the video teases people or notifies them about your merchandise.

This is not simple since you need to do it in an attention-grabbing manner, however, if you manage to give this sufficient time, you could develop a nice specific title that is going to get folks thrilled about your niche-specific social media account.

## Develop Niche-Targeted Descriptions or Commentary for Curated Content

Not just should you recreate the title of the material which you're poaching, but you ought to likewise do the identical for its commentary or descriptions.

It's truly vital to render it obvious that this content is planned for a particular audience. In this manner, when this material bursts its way all across the web and across all social media networks, it could then screen people who have an interest in the content. Only folks who are truly in your niche would wish to visit the link which you combined with the content to go back to your social network account.

## Utilize Niche-Targeted Hashtags

This bit of advice relates to folks utilizing curated content on Instagram and Twitter. In case you did your homework properly in Chapter 4 and 5, you ought to already take note of Twitter hashtags which are well-known in your niche.

Assemble a list of these. Revolve among these whenever you post curated content on Twitter and Instagram. By doing this, you "piggyback" on hashtags being browsed for by folks interested in your niche. This is the way you acquire niche-targeted eyeballs.

Again, the entire idea here is not just to drive a crowd of typically uninterested folks to your social media accounts. Rather, you're aiming to get a good flow of folks who are really interested in your niche, and after that getting them to follow you on social media.

## Don't Forget the Secondary Impacts of Curated Viral Content

Viral content is so effective since you don't just draw in folks who are already intrigued by your niche, you likewise find yourself encouraging them to share with their personal social circles. This may lead people sharing identical interests, or nearly identical interests, to notice the links to your social media accounts.

So recognize how this secondary traffic impact operates when creating titles, commentary and descriptions. You're not merely repackaging trendy content. You're attempting to get to folks and also their friends and the friends of those friends who partake in the identical niche interests.

I wish to provide you this broad view so you can see how vital this is. This is not a thing you just waft through. So you need to give this appropriate focus so as to make the most of the niche targeting capabilities of the curated viral material which you are sharing.

## Chapter 7: Don't Forget to Take Certain Precautions When Sharing Other People's Content

### Remember to Protect Yourself When Sharing Others' Content

I wish I could inform you that you can easily flat out reuse everybody's material without any judicial problems. Obviously, if I were to say that to you, I would be lying.

In case you are intending to be curating tried and verified viral material, you need to legally protect yourself. How do you accomplish this?

### The power of the CTTO

What does CTTO mean? It means 'Credit To The Owner.' The moment you post this, you are stating to the world that you don't own the content and that you are crediting ownership to the individual who really owns the material Now, recognize that when people publish CTTO, they don't simply accomplish it in passing.

The ones who accomplish this properly are going to link to the source. For instance, in case you are publishing a funny cat video and it appears that it was a video initially made famous by an individual with a personal account, feature their personal account hyperlink in your curated post. Set CTTO and after that the link to that individual.

By doing this, people would understand that the individual is the owner. You are simply curating this material. This is a really vital aspect of getting legal protection. You need to give proper acknowledgment. You can not give the perception that you developed this content on your own.

**Ensure to Comment on the Content**

Within US copyright law along with Canadian intellectual property law, in case you utilize other people's secured intellectual property, you can obtain a bit of protection for lawsuits when you perform particular things. First off, your posting of the content needs to have some kind of commentary. Either you're sharing it for novel value or you're sharing it to encourage discussion.

This is just how the fair use doctrine functions. It is all about uncovering copyright law to enable authentic discussion. By doing this, whenever you comment, you are activating the fair use doctrine. Now, I'm not claiming that your comment ought to be very brief and superficial. That's most likely not going to save you.

In case you will be curating other folks' viral material, your comment needs to be content in of itself. It has to be that valuable. It needs to have some kind of effect and it practically must contribute value to the content which you are curating. You can't simply say, "Take a look at this" or "Haha, hilarious." That's not going to do the job.

Use this incredible opportunity to discuss your niche. Use this chance to emphasize your competence and degree of authority in your niche. By doing this, you will kill two birds with one stone. Also, you qualify the curated content within the fair use doctrine. This renders it tougher for the content owner to take legal action against you for copyright infringement.

Bear in mind, within international intellectual property law, the only individual who can hand out the copies of his or her original work is the content creator. Additionally, that individual might designate those rights to another individual. Those are the only folks who possess legal rights within copyright law.

The fair use doctrine ensures exemptions in particular contexts concerning that protection. By doing this, you can openly share someone's content, given that you are including commentary, providing value or you are arranging it to foster conversation.

It is likewise crucial to ensure that the content which you are sharing is not the entire content. For instance, you are most likely going to bump into problems if you share a complete movie which someone else makes. However, if you will share bits of the screenshots or video such as the things which you see on Buzzfeed, you most likely are going to be fine.

You need to check out how much of the content you are sampling or quoting. In case you utilize the entire content, then you might find yourself in trouble. It is also vital that you link to the source. By doing this, they profit from your curation. This creates a win-win scenario.

In many cases, third-party content creators truly don't mind. Actually, they would like to encourage you. How come? The more you spread their material, the more traffic they receive. The more you promote their content, the better their brand ends up being. You're doing them a huge favor. Things get a tad tricky when you're sharing bits of well-known films or TV shows. That's when things might get a bit touchy.

Do yourself a huge favor and see to it that there is a commentary along with the material that you are curating. See to it that you utilize the phrase CTTO to protect yourself. Additionally, if you receive any sort of complaint or notice from the rights owner, take the curated content down. It's simply not worth it. You don't wish to muck up all the money that you have managed to accumulate, creating your own unique online brand, due to the fact that you don't wish to let go of curated content.

In case you're accomplishing this right, you ought to have a bunch of curated materials either way. You're not truly losing a lot if the rights owner informs you to take down a couple of posts on your social media accounts. When you receive such notifications, ensure you act on them immediately. Don't sleep on them. You're just going to be making things more difficult on yourself in case they make a decision to take legal action against you.

Make no mistake, intellectual property right law is serious. There are penalties which you can encounter and you could even spend jail time. It may become that terrible, so do yourself a huge favor and see to it you secure yourself sufficiently when sharing other folks' content.

Now, please recognize that what makes this truly muddy is the reality that whenever content goes viral on the web, it typically changes hands numerous times. As a matter of fact, this might have occurred so much that you truly don't recognize who the actual owner is. You truly don't understand who developed that content originally.

Do yourself a huge favor and see to it that you comply with the guidelines above and you are really receptive to take down notifications or alerts.

## Chapter 8: Sharing Viral Content on Facebook

## How do You Share Viral Content on Facebook

Now that you possess a great comprehension of your splendid approach for sharing viral content and taking advantage of content curation to develop your social networks and blog following, here is a particular chapter on viral content advertising on Facebook.

## Publish Viral Content First on Your Facebook Page

The initial thing which you want to do is to publish the curated content on your Facebook page. This is the starting point at which you're going to publish your content. You then go on the link of that created post and republish other sections on Facebook along with Twitter and other social media networks utilizing tools such as HootSuite.

This convenient tool allowed you to upload a large quantity of content to your social media accounts and stretch out the publishing of that content. You could additionally experiment with the comments, hashtags, and headlines. The fantastic thing about HootSuite is you don't need to babysit your social media accounts, telling it when it ought to post.

You just want to assign the time and prepare the software and basically forget it. As soon as you have submitted all your content, you can practically just kick back and let HootSuite do its thing. Whenever folks check out your social media accounts, they sense that you're actively running your account since you're posting at a regular pace.

What they don't understand is that you have in fact set this up well ahead of time and it was the program that posted this content. This is a fantastic way of automating your procedures so you don't need to physically or personally do the work. A great deal of folks actually generate wonderful passive income just by utilizing tools such as HootSuite to upload curated content on their social media accounts.

These then direct traffic to their mailing lists. These lists are then set up to deliver promotions at certain times. The owners and users of these systems just kick back and accumulate cash. I know, it seems quite amazing, but you need to have a system in addition to an unmistakable plan if you want to pull this off.

## When Should you Republish

In case you carried out your homework properly, you ought to have a substantial assortment of viral content in your niche. This stuff is a science. These pieces of content are recognized to draw in a remarkable amount of eyeballs in your niche. The issue is, you don't wish to maintain republishing the identical content repeatedly.

For instance, in case you have 300 links and you have put together HootSuite to tweet out your content at a rate of 6 times per day, this implies that after 50 days, your list is going to get reposted once more. You might wish to tweet more often, such as 12 times a day, and this would lower your repost date to 25 days.

Can you notice the issue here? You're most likely going to forfeit followers if it ends up apparent to them that you're simply reusing the identical content repeatedly, this is why I recommend that you get a substantial quantity of material so that even though you are posting at a very frequent rate each and each day, your reposting won't appear apparent.

## Why Bother Reposting?

You can accomplish things the difficult way and obtain just an enormous list of content and establish your system to ensure that you are never going to post the same material more than once. You're welcome to do so. It requires a great deal of work, time and energy. A bunch of people don't do things this way. Rather, they prefer to repost.

Provided that you have sufficient material to reuse, you ought to be fine. In case you're going to be reposting one time every two months, that ought to be secure. Still, why should you repost? Well, when you accomplish this, you get numerous pieces of the pie. Maybe for whatever reason, your original post did not acquire your followers' awareness, hey, it happens sometimes. In case you repost, you get another opportunity.

Also, whenever viral content becomes popular, it gets cold really fast, but this doesn't always indicate that folks who were initially curious about it have entirely lost all interest. Whenever you repost at a later date, you may stir up interest. Folks might assume that it's a wonderful throwback and share it and this may give you fresh fans.

Irrespective, if sufficient time has elapsed since you initially posted the curated content, you provide your fans with the perception that they are discovering fresh content. This is always a benefit.

## Regularly Incorporate a Link to Your Landing Page With Your Curated Viral Material

Each time you post curated viral content, you ought to link to the source, you need to give appropriate acknowledgment, but you ought to likewise link to your conversion page. This is your mailing list. If you can't accomplish that, then Facebook is going to post your curated material as something posted by your Facebook page.

This could be adequate. In case you are sharing the direct post on your Facebook page to corresponding Facebook groups or additional pages, folks may click to like your page and perhaps receive your updates.

## Post Your Facebook Pages' URLs on Niche-related Facebook Groups

Now that you have released a bunch of material on your Facebook page, take the links of those posts and share them on Facebook groups in the identical niche. Now, please recognize that you can not undertake this on the first day. You can't simply enroll in a group and suddenly begin sharing links. You're going to seem like a spammer. Folks certainly won't appreciate what you're doing.

You most likely are going to get banned sooner as opposed to later. I recommend that you don't even attempt to do so. Rather, register with these niche-related Facebook groups and interact with group members. Ask a bunch of questions, let them know what you know and typically carry yourself like a recognized participant of the community.

Keep in mind, these Facebook groups are just internet message boards. They resemble small online communities. Whenever you participate in these places, carry yourself like an accountable community member. Provide value to the discussions via your posts. This is the way in which you develop credibility.

When you have set up trustworthiness and authority, you would then have the ability to share a portion of your content along with the direct third-party links which you're sharing. You ought to do this to cover your tracks. You don't wish to be apparent with regards to this. Folks can easily notice that you are simply advertising your Facebook page. Folks don't appreciate that. It's just a question of time until they ban you.

If you're intending to be dropping links, a tiny portion of that ought to be your Facebook page, but the large majority ought to be high-quality material. It truly encourages discussion. That's how you establish authority and how you are given more consent to keep publishing your own stuff. you need to earn this by becoming reputable first.

## Facebook Viral Content Approach

In case I haven't been obvious yet. Allow me to spell it out. For Facebook, your viral content approach needs to initially involve posting your curated viral material on your Facebook page. Subsequently, you share that content on niche-related groups. This is going to then push likes to your Facebook page. You wish for Facebook users to end up on your page.

By providing ample information, a portion of them may like the page and this indicates that any time you post an update, a certain portion of your page fans may notice your content. This could then result in those folks noticing your sales page links and ending up on your website or your squeeze page.

Afterward, auto-publish content on your Facebook page to make the most of eyeballs on your sales page. Simply put, keep posting regularly to your Facebook page. Don't feel bad about this. Please recognize that only a small fraction of your Facebook fans are going to get to notice your updates.

The large bulk of folks who have liked your page are not going to notice your updates unless they pick the option "see first" the moment they initially like your page. But speaking generally, just a tiny portion of your page fans are going to see your updates, so it really aid to post regularly and to publish a good deal.

Provided that the quality is there and provided the quality is good enough to foster interaction, you ought to not struggle with this. However, in case you just post stuff that has positively no engagement, Facebook may effectively penalize you. In case you believe very few of your fans are noticing your content presently, wait until Facebook penalizes you for low engagement. Even less fans are going to notice your content following the penalty.

Next, acquire clicks on your sales page. This is the way you acquire list members. Lastly, you auto-publish your email updates and you receive conversions passively. That's the way you play ball. You essentially just send email updates to your mailing list on an automated schedule. That's the way you direct traffic to post with advertisements or you receive traffic to actual sales pages.

In case you're offering your own products and they purchase anything, you receive 100% of whatever cash they spent. Map out your general Facebook viral approach utilizing the pattern I described above.

# Chapter 9: Sharing Viral Content on Twitter

## How to Share Viral Content on Twitter

Publish the viral Twitter content on your Twitter timeline. After you have published the current viral content video or hyperlink or image, tag prominent profiles in your niche. These are folks who currently follow this kind of content. Tag them to obtain their attention. In case you've carried out your research properly, you ought to recognize who these folks are.

Odds are, you are syndicating a bit their content at the same time. Also, by this point, you currently understand what sort of niche-related hashtags people curious about your kind of content might use. Utilize these hashtags. The key here is to utilize HootSuite or any other kind of auto-publishing resource to revolve your hashtag.

I can not stress this sufficiently. You need to revolve your hashtags. Why? Whenever folks have an interest in a certain niche or a certain small range of subjects, they utilize hashtags. There resemble the search engine keyword terms you are pinpointing. The issue is, you don't have an idea which hashtags are going to direct the most traffic. You're totally in the dark.

This is the reason why you need to revolve your hashtags. At some point, when you take a look at your statistics and you check out the timing of the traffic originating from Twitter, you should manage to link the dots. You ought to have the ability to take an educated guess as to which particular hashtag set made up the lovely search and traffic.

Don't overlook revolving your hashtags. Failure to accomplish so will be an overlooked possibility. You're going to be making a mistake big time in case you don't bother to revolve hashtags. You ought to already understand what hashtags are popular in your niche. It's a great idea to keep gathering hashtag ideas and revolving among them to find which ones really generate the most results.

## Fill your Twitter Feed Using Auto-publishing Resources Like HootSuite

The great thing about HootSuite is that you are able to utilize a database file utilizing the CSV format to enter content data. You don't need to by hand enter every bit of content that you wish HootSuite to post for you.

In case you're using MS Excel and storing it as a CSV, ensure that you are revolving your hashtags. See to it that you are 'resharing' or retweeting specific material and then revolve the hashtags. Even in case you are not retweeting curated content, you ought to still revolve your hashtags.

Again, the trick here is to regularly try things out to notice which hashtag truly accounts for the lovely rise of traffic your sales page has received.

## Do This While Auto-publishing

While HootSuite is carrying out its thing, you should not just kick back, kick back and expect the cash to arrive. I know that's what a bunch of "make money online" books or "online marketing riches" books tell you to expect. That's the buzz. That's certainly the dream. Sadly, dreams are frequently very different from the truth.

In case you wish for your curated viral material social media network marketing strategy to be effective, you need to wrap your sleeves and do something on the side. Although your stuff is auto-publishing, search for competitors' profiles on Twitter. You ought to already possess a list of these. Check out their followers and take note of the most engaged ones.

These are the ones which are essentially tweeting each and every day and after that screen them based upon their niche specificity. Check out their Twitter feeds. What do these followers typically tweet about? In case you can see a tight connection between your material and the things that they are regularly tweeting or retweeting, follow them.

This is important. Follow them. Here is how this could result in you acquiring more followers on

Twitter. Typically speaking, when individuals follow other profiles, a particular percentage of the folks they follow is going to in turn follow them back. This is "follow me and I follow you." It all comes down to reciprocity.

Now, this should not be shocking. It goes without saying, when you behave well towards someone, the odds are fairly good that they are going to be nice back to you. That's the way the human brain is wired. Whenever folks follow you back instantly on Twitter, that's simply reciprocity at work in the digital realm. This is a really strong kind of promotion due to the fact that the folks following you back are more probable to be in your niche target market.

These are individuals who are more likely to be really curious about what you have to share. At some point, they might continue noticing your sales page tweets enough times that they become involved. Just keep in mind that the component of the reason why the overall number of clickthroughs on Twitter is fairly low contrasted to other social media networks is due to the rule of 8.

Simply put, folks get so saturated with a lot of information on Twitter that they essentially need to keep seeing the identical bit of content repeatedly for them to assume that it's fine to click on it. In their heads, outright familiarity implies that in some way the content is rather credible to take a chance on that content.

No matter what the case might be, continue retweeting your stuff utilizing tools such as HootSuite while simultaneously directly following involved followers of your competition.

## Concentrate on the Strategy

It is truly vital to ensure that you auto-publish just niche-specific viral content. You ought to already recognize this, but in case you are still unclear on the concept, you need to see to it that all the curated content which you are creating are on point. They must be niche specific.

Also, they need to be tried and verified, or else they have previously been retweeted and shared. This is second-hand stuff. This is not stuff that someone just created. This is content that has been moving around since you recognize folks have an interest in this stuff.

Next, you develop an organic following of niche-specific followers by means of reverse engineering your competitors' following by merely looking at your competitors, checking out their follower count and cherry-picking their most niche-specific engaged followers.

In case your stuff is really niche-specific and you make it a goal to provide value to the lives of folks looking into your content, don't be amazed that a comparatively high percentage of folks you followed will wind up following you back. Nitty-gritty here is to obtain niche followers making use of niche-specific content.

This might boost the odds of you making it with your sales page material. Obviously, nothing is promised, but in the event that you follow all the actions mentioned above and your followers are extremely niche focused, your odds of transforming

these folks into actual customers could be quite
high.

## Chapter 10: How Content Formats Can Help You Go Viral

## Filter Your Content Formats to Get Viral on Numerous Platforms

By just getting content from one platform and after that sharing it on a different one, you can get fairly good flow of traffic. Now, please recognize as I pointed out at least twice within this book, even if a bit of content is popular on one platform doesn't immediately imply that it is going to gain footing in another. Always keep in mind that.

With that being said, here are certain prevalent strategies for 'resharing' content from one platform to another.

### YouTube Video Approach

The initial thing which you want to do is to discover YouTube videos which have a substantial amount of views. This is the initial sign of success. This video is not some sleeper video. It's not a video which was posted and was promptly forgotten. This video, in fact, gets a great deal of attention in your YouTube niche.

Afterward, take note of the comments. How many comments are there? Typically, whenever people post a comment, it indicates that they are sentimentally invested in the video. It either got through to them on a certain level or it touched them in a certain way. Whatever the case might be, it had an effect on them. Try to find high comment videos and, ultimately, check out the number of likes.

This is not as vital as the amount of comments and the amount of views. Once more, you want to double-check that these YouTube videos which you're thinking about reposting are truly specific to your niche. As soon as you are that this is the type of video you might wish to curate, download these and share on your Twitter and Facebook profiles.

Again, see to it to secure yourself by featuring CTTO and linking to the YouTube channel of the origin. Whenever sharing on Twitter, revolve the hashtag. In a similar way, you are able to download Twitter and Facebook video material and share on your YouTube channel. You're essentially just carrying out things in reverse.

However, you will need to secure yourself by posting an acknowledgment link beside the CTTO text.

**Image Strategy**

Locate viral infographic or image material on Pinterest and Instagram. Share these on Twitter and Facebook with suitable acknowledgment. Do the identical with viral Facebook and Twitter image content, but on the Pinterest and Instagram networks. Again, ensure you revolve your hashtags. See to it that this stuff is truly niche specific.

Additionally, in case you discover viral content in your niche on Facebook and Twitter, search for accounts on Instagram and Pinterest that pinpoint those niches. Check out their followers and attempt to follow those supporters and perhaps get them to follow you back. By doing this, you're focusing on two levels. You're not simply shuffling curated material all over. You're likewise expanding an organic niche following for your profiles.

## All Content Must Ultimately Take to Your Conversion Accounts

On your YouTube channel, you ought to have a hyperlink to your squeeze page or website. This might be within your about page. This might also be in the explanation of each video you upload on YouTube. Please recognize that the majority of people don't check out the about link on YouTube. They may like your videos, but they may not make an effort to get more details about you.

Do yourself a huge favor and see to it that each time you post a video, place your squeeze page link or website link in the description segment.

## Twitter Approach

On your Twitter profile, ensure you feature your squeeze page link or your website link in your bio account and revolve among these in the material which you are sharing. The identical relates to your Facebook page, in addition to your Facebook group posts. It's all about making the most of eyeballs to your squeeze page or your website homepage.

Naturally, as I've pointed out numerous times here, when you are reposing curated content, you need to be hands-on. You can't simply take content which is presently popular and merely shuffle it off to a different network or redistribute it on the identical network that content is currently on. You're most likely not going to gain a whole lot from that content's viral allure.

You need to experiment with the headline, in addition to the commentary, and truly provide more value to each part of the content. As you could most likely tell, this could require quite a long time and that is the reason why I recommend that you work with a virtual assistant with sound English skills from places such as Fiverr or in case you're aiming to save cash, cognoplus.com.

If you require professional writing services, you may wish to have a go at Upwork or if you are running on a budget but require really high quality, have a go at ozki.org.

## Conclusion of Viral Marketing

This guide hands out numerous tricks that you most likely haven't heard about before. There is a reason why these tricks are not exposed. They are not popular. A bunch of folks who make their living encouraging others that they can easily transform into immediate overnight millionaires doing internet marketing don't want you to learn about these tricks.

They don't wish for you to find out about the effort involved. They don't wish for you to understand that there is a faster way. They don't wish for you to learn about the reality that you can shrink your road to success by just reverse engineering other individuals' success. They don't wish for you to recognize the truth that you could utilize your competitors to perform your due diligence for you.

They wish to maintain you in the dark regarding all of that. Why would they wish to do it? Well, they want you to think that in case you produce sought-after material, folks are going to magically show up on your site. Basically, they want you to continue returning to them for advice. They don't really wish to give you the pure framework you require so you could get going.

Now, please be aware that I'm offering you a pure framework. You still must continuously experiment, fine-tune and change whatever it is you are doing to improve your circumstances. This allows you to fine-tune your outcomes and inevitably attain ultimate success. When dealing with viral content, it truly all comes down to discovering what works and building on it.

In the event that this is your attitude, you really ought to succeed. However, if you believe that you simply have to poach other people's project and invest very little time and work in syndicating this content, you most likely will not be too successful. Keep in mind, eventually, everything comes down to the value you contribute to people's lives.

That is the bottom line. In case you implement all the recommendations and tricks which I've provided within this guide with value in mind, you really ought to wind up doing really good. I wish you nothing except the ultimate success.

# Laptop Lifestyle

Use Digital Marketing to Make Money Online Which Will Enable You to Create Your Ultimate Lifestyle of Time and Location Independence

By Adam Torbert

## Introduction to Laptop Lifestyle

There are numerous articles about people who make a decision to start blogging or doing SEO and about how to improve those skills. There is another important topic that gets a lot less coverage, which is how a person can be positively impacted by being able to do work online. Working online can benefit someone's personal development. This can manifest in a myriad of ways and someone's attitude and mental state can be affected in many ways. If you are interested in this, then digital marketing may just be the career for you.

The fact is that jobs do have an impact on us. Anything you do has an impact on you, even blogging. If you do something such as blogging, then the chances are high that you don't have that many colleagues whom you can be more like, which does leave its mark on you. Being able to work from home can certainly have an impact on people as well. Blogging and SEO may be different than regular jobs, but it still changes a person in some way. However, it is necessary to have a modicum of self-awareness in order to notice this and to precisely know what had changed.

I can say with certainty that I am a lot more carefree and less rigid in comparison to my other friends who have normal jobs. People who have regular jobs tend to get really stressed if they happen to stay up way past their imposed bedtime. I, on the other hand, have more flexibility which means that I get to decide when and I work and when I don't. This can make things frustrating when you can't get people to hang out with you since they have to work the following day. The longer this goes on, the more detached you tend to become of the world and the people who have standard routines.

When you write online on a regular basis, you tend to get opinionated. It is not unusual to be opinionated on a certain topic, but it can be easier to express oneself and share opinions online. This is the benefit of having more freedom.

Working online can increase your confidence, which is something that always comes in handy. When you know that you can make money online, you get the feeling and the realization that there is so much more than you can possibly manage to do. This will contribute to you feeling like you are a success which can lead to you accomplishing your short term and long term goals. Increased independence makes you more self-reliant if you are the kind of person who can manage their time and projects effectively.

These are just some ways in which you can expect to be changed as a digital marketer. The exact changes will depend on your current situation, however. In any case, you can expect to grow and change a whole lot from the experience of getting into digital marketing.

## Chapter 1: What You Need to Know About Digital Marketing

Most people get into digital marketing with the goal of improving their lives in more ways than one. There is also a good chance that online gurus sold you a dream of an easy life once you got into the digital marketing space.

When you work in digital marketing, you work online and anywhere, without a supervisor. That is what can make life much more pleasant. Being able to pick your hours and your location is a blessing. Everything you have to do, you can do on your own without anyone breathing down your neck and complaining if things aren't being done completely according to their plan.

The great thing about digital marketing is the fact that it can enable you to earn passive income, therefore earning money while you sleep. This passive income can come from various sources, such as websites or a Youtube channel. After you have done the initial work, the fruits of your labor will continue sending the rewards your way. This means that you can take a break whenever you want since your money and your time aren't directly correlated.

You can also accomplish all of this by focusing on topics that you care about and that you have a passion for. These are the things you don't mind getting up early for. This is the ideal of being a digital marketer, making good money following your dreams. You may be wondering, at this point, why isn't everyone doing this kind of thing?

The truth of the matter is that things are more complicated than it may initially seem. The reality of things is that the majority of people don't wake up to a website which is drowning in traffic and generating passive income. Not many people are successful in achieving that and such a goal requires a lot of time.

Building a sizeable email list takes time and patience, but that is what you need if you intend to make money from things such as affiliate marketing. It takes so much time due to the fact that the website won't blow up overnight.

Acquiring the necessary knowledge and skills also takes time. Anyone starting off with digital marketing won't know what they are doing and they are likely to get overwhelmed. Mistakes are inevitable. The first brand someone builds may end up being quite embarrassing.

Anyone not sharing the spot on the top of the digital marketing industry is likely to scrap their first few business ventures. The only thing that can be done at that point is cutting the losses and moving on and trying to be better next time. It doesn't really matter how many times you fail, you only have to hit it big once.

It is helpful knowing that none of the big names in the internet marketing space got things right the first time. It is necessary to keep going and not to get discouraged since you are learning a lot from trying different things. This is the part of digital marketing which is difficult and not necessarily fun.

A lot of gurus probably sold you a dream that you can quit your job just like that and start living the laptop lifestyle. Because of all those promises, you worked and worked and worked, staying up late and neglecting other areas of your life, just to get nothing in return. This kind of thing can be really soul-crushing.

The truth about passive income is the fact that true passive income is hard to achieve and a lot of online entrepreneurs don't quite get there. The fact is that they make a lot of active income by doing work for clients. In some cases, working for clients can be like having a boss. No matter how nice a certain client will be, he will expect the delivery of results according to deadlines.

Doing the work which you don't like is unavoidable eventually, such as writing about topics you don't care about even slightly and designing websites for such topics. On top of all that, there is a chance you won't get paid on time, or that the money simply won't come in when in between clients.

Working at home also may not be what it is cracked up to be and it may be easy to lose your mind. No matter how well you design your environment and no matter how driven and disciplined you are, the temptation to procrastinate and to indulge in short term pleasures will always be there.

It can also be common for the work to bleed into the time which you would spend on other things since you just can't get yourself to stop working. The temptation to fill the gaps with a bit more work is always there. If you are getting paid based on results, then you will always be tempted to do a bit more work.

When working like this, the money you will be getting will always be going up and down and it can be difficult to plan ahead for the finances when you can never be sure about how much money will be coming in. You also have to deal with your taxes and just thinking about it may make you anxious.

All these things are addressed throughout this book. There are two types of people when it comes to handling these kinds of things. The first type is the person who looks and feels like a million bucks. Their grooming is on point, they dress with intention, they talk with conviction and they travel and enjoy life. It is quite easy to see why these people are paid so highly.

Then there is the other type. This person is constantly overworked  and is barely above broke. Their minds is working far below its capacity due to being overworked and stressed out, which makes it harder for them to give the proper time and attention to their lives as a whole.

The second type is a lot more common, and the goal of this book is to make sure that the reader ends up in the former category. Time to get started!

## Chapter 2:  Money VS Work-Life Balance

There is no better way to start this chapter than by
mentioning the classic: The 4 Hour Work Week by
Tim Ferris. The 4 Hour Work Week is a book which
achieved a lot of success teaching people about
lifestyle design. The lifestyle design boils down to
designing your life according to things that matter
to you instead of being stuck in the system. This
means leveraging the system to your advantage,
which can put you in the position of having more
time and money.

The book certainly had an impact and it created an
entire movement of digital nomads. Digital nomads
are people who leverage technology to work from
anywhere, which can give them the freedom to have
more experiences across the world. The main
audience of this book are entrepreneurs and online
marketers. The truth is that the principles within
that book could be applied by anyone to achieve
great results.

No matter what knowing some financial tips can
dramatically change the course of your life, even if
you are working in an office and are content with it.

In the book, Tim Ferris shows the reader how not all
money is made the same. The majority of people
think that measuring wealth boils down to how
much dollars are made over the course of longer
periods of time, such as months and years. Tim
advises that most people start focusing on how

much money they make per hour. This is focusing on relative income.

For example, if someone makes 5000 USD per month working two days per week, that person is relatively wealthier than a person earning 15000 USD per month, working each and every day of the week. By doing some math, you could easily see that the first person makes a lot more money per hour and that they have a lot more attractive ratio between money and freedom.

Simply earning money aimlessly shouldn't be the only goal. The goal should be knowing how much money is necessary to afford a desired lifestyle and to realize how to get to the position of earning that amount of money in a time-efficient manner. If you are so overburdened that you can't drop everything to go out for a walk, then you are doing things wrong. Isn't the main point of money enabling more freedom and choices?

A lot of people wanting to work online make mistakes here. Anyone who is selling and offering their services online has a strong temptation to work more in order to earn more. Working more hours in order to bring in more cash can work in the short term, but it is necessary to take a moment to reflect on things. People who have regular jobs work 8 hours a day on average. If you work 12 hours per day, you may end up earning less per hour than someone with a regular job.

You want to position yourself so that the system works in your favor. How is this achieved? The first thing that likely comes to mind is setting up a web-based business of some kind with the hope of creating passive income streams from assets. Those assets can range from selling an app to selling an ebook. If you don't want to do the heavy lifting, you can also look into dropshipping, where the production and the delivery of the product is done by a third party. Needless to say, there are quite a few avenues of earning passive income.

Before we move on, it is necessary to clarify the difference between salary and wealth. It is also advised to shift the thinking into not measuring success by income alone. This is what most people think of first when they think of success.

A lot of people working standard jobs are under the impression that the only way to move up the wealth ladder is by asking for a raise or getting a higher paying job. In reality, wealth is measured by the money you have saved up and stashed in the bank. You could be working at Mcdonalds earning minimum wage, and still be wealthy by inhering millions from a deceased relative.

Decreasing your expenses could also be one way to increase your wealth. You could accomplish this by moving into smaller living space or by moving to an area where living expenses are lower, such as the countryside. One additional way is by spending less money on groceries and clothes. This essentially boils down to downgrading your lifestyle, but that is how you can put some cash to the side, which can make you feel pretty secure.

If you work online, then packing up and moving to another country entirely is as easy as it gets. A lot of savvy people tend to take advantage of geo arbitrage and moving to more tropical countries where they can afford luxury goods at a fraction of the price.

If you want to live the high life, you can spend every penny you earn and take out loans and get into debt in order to pay for everything you want so that you can look successful, even though the numbers say the contrary.

The choice is yours, but I think that nothing material that you can purchase with money compares to freedom, not even close. It all boils down to having the self-awareness to know what you value and what you find important. Before you start anything, be aware of the lifestyle you want and knowing what you have to do and how much money you need to make that lifestyle into a reality. That is what the lifestyle design philosophy is all about.

To start off, do some math and figure out the amount of money you need to earn daily. If your calculations show that the minimum amount of money you need daily is 100 USD, then you want to work until you earn that amount which would allow you to cover your basic living expenses. If you want to afford something extra such as gadgets or eating out, then you may have to work a little past that minimum monetary amount. Everyone has to figure their own targets out in order to know how much needs to be done.

## Chapter 3: Passion or Reality?

Most internet marketers begin with a dream in mind. They start off with a belief and they want to do what it takes in order to be successful. There is a good chance you have an idea for a successful website. Maybe you are really into video games and you want to earn a living by blogging about it. The other possibility is that you just like using technology in order to achieve something.

Regardless, you are starting off with the end in mind and you have an idea of what success looks like to you. However, it will take time until you will actually be able to generate an income from doing that.

Ultimately, there are two options: You can try doing what you love in the hope of great success one day in the future. The second option is focusing on something that is guaranteed to generate some money even though you might not care about the work so much. The truth of the matter is that both of these options are wrong routes to take.

If you go with the first option, then you will be focusing on your website and your email list with the goal of growing them. If you keep working on this, then there will be growth, but it will be slow and it won't be something which will allow you to afford a worthwhile lifestyle. It is the fact that most people don't have the patience or the discipline to see this through until the end.

If you pick the second option, then you will likely never have time to do what you are passionate about. You will likely be too busy doing client work. If you work on other people's projects, then you will likely never get around to doing your own projects which means that you might have to pay someone else to do the work for your website.

When things are organized in such a way, it can be very easy to reach the limit of what can be realistically done in a day after which things don't really change and you get a feeling of being in a rat race. The longer this lasts, the more loathing you have towards your projects and burnout just keeps inching closer and closer.

Is there a solution for this? Is there a way out? It all goes back to knowing how much money you need to earn per day. This is your daily goal and after achieving it, then you can start focusing on your own needs without any guilt or worry.

The first part of the day should be spent doing client work, such as SEO and website design. This is the stuff that brings in the money and that you don't necessarily have an interest in. Once you have hit your monetary goal doing these activities, then you can focus on other things.

Over time you will be able to estimate how long it takes to do the necessary work and you will be able to create time blocks based on that. The first part of the day should be spent doing the necessary work. Once that part is over, then it is possible to work on the stuff you really want to work on and which has the potential to take your career to another level entirely.

What was described above is the concept of bootstrapping, which allows you to fund your own projects without debt or any outside funding. A lot of people are hesitant to go into digital marketing because they think it can't be done without a loan. How things are in reality is quite different.

If you want to go after your goal of achieving the dream lifestyle, what you can do in the beginning is starting a project on the side. If you are doing things such as SEO or web design, then it is safe to say that you are someone who wants to be creative and forward think and that you are someone who doesn't avoid risks in life. The willingness to utilize the technologies that is available in order to create the life you want is certainly admirable. This goal cant be accomplished without having a variety of skills.

If this describes you, then you are aware of the need to push yourself on a regular basis so that you could familiarize yourself with technologies which exist and skills which are important. The more time you spend learning and practicing, the more opportunities will be available to you, which will enable you to achieve more success. In order to accomplish this, taking on a project on the side is the right thing to do.

Even when you start moving up the ranks as a digital marketer, there will always be a need to have projects on the side. The side project is anything other than your main money-making ventures. This is what you dedicate your extra time, whether you work for yourself or a regular 9 to 5 job. The main reason for doing these side projects is the necessary skill development for getting ahead.

On top of that, you may earn something that would serve as a secondary income source. Even if you don't earn any money to brag about, you will end up learning a lot of valuable skills which will be very useful in taking you to the next level.

Not all side projects are good and it is necessary to know how to choose a side project that is in the domain of your main career, which would also allow you to develop your skills further. If someone is a web designer, then a good side project for that person would be something that would teach that person how to be a better coder or how to be a better digital artist. This is also good since it will give you an opportunity to not have your mind constantly on your main job.

For example, if you are working with anything that has to do with design, such as apps and websites, then it makes perfect sense to learn about app development as a part of the holistic approach. When you start doing this, you will find that the whole process is actually quite fun. The potential for making money is also there and there are many ways to accomplish that.

YouTube also warrants mentioning since it can be a really lucrative opportunity for someone who knows what to do. A couple of videos can be all that is required to gain some following and to leverage that to start bringing in some profit. This can be pretty fun while also providing an opportunity for even more marketing.

As far as blogs are concerned, what topic you decide to center your blog around is likely going to be a hot topic that would give you the best chances of monetizing your blog and therefore making it your main thing. Still, there is a chance that working on this blog won't be your favorite thing in the world and that is why running your personal blog separately could be a good idea. If that doesn't succeed, you will at least have had some fun. On the other hand, if it does end up being successful, you could end up with another source of income.

Once again, what you should do is to have something which you are working on as a main avenue of making money, while working on your dream project on the side which can enable you to make a living as long as you stick with it.

What to do if you can't decide on an idea? Maybe you know that you want to be successful, but you are not sure what to do exactly. If you are into digital marketing, the chances are that you have multiple ideas when it comes to websites you could create. You probably don't just have potential ideas for websites, but also for ebooks, applications and all other kinds of assets which could make you money and bring you success.

The issue is that having too many things requiring your attention means that you won't be able to focus on either of those things properly. There are only so many hours in a day and there is a limit to how much time you can dedicate to working on your project. You also have to keep bringing money in, no matter what.

If there is an inability to stick to an idea, then that is an issue and the issue has nothing to do with motivation and discipline. The fact is that deciding which project to focus is hard. If you have way too many ideas that are requiring your attention, then you will find it hard to  stay focused on a current idea due to being distracted by the following idea.

To make things even harder, something like building a website does take time and it can be quite boring at times. The idea of creating a successful website is certainly an exciting one, but after spending time with search engine optimization and aligning each CSS code, it can be quite easy for the enthusiasm to drop.

Things that you are interested in change over time and that is a perfectly normal thing. One month you may be really into books, and then, all of sudden, its all about videogames. What you will be inspired to write about will most likely be the thing that interests you at that particular time.

So what do you do in order to tackle this problem? Should you choose one thing and then stick with it until it is done? One option is to write down the potential benefits of all the projects that seem interesting to you. You are obviously doing this to make money, but just looking at money isnt the solution, even though its a start. What you should pay attention to is the likely length of the project until it reaches its completion.

A website about crossfit may be something you would love to create, but the chances of success could be a lot lower if there happens to be a lot of competition. You may have better odds creating a new social media platform, but it would require a lot of investment and knowledge about topics such as programming. What you should aim for is a smaller niche which you have an interest in. The niche should be about something that interests you, starting should be relatively easy and it should be something that could bring in return on investment fairly quickly.

The same goes for any other form of passive income such as making money from ebooks on Amazon.

The requirement is that money from the opportunity starts coming in soon after the completion of the project, after which there is no need for constant, continual time investment. If those criteria are met, then you should knock out that project quickly so that you could start receiving residual gains as soon as you can.

You can decide which project has the best chances to put money in your pocket the quickest and based on that you can know how to best direct your time and energy. The ultimate goal of this is you not having to spend as much time on the necessities, which means that you can dedicate more time towards other projects.

In a situation where you simply can't decide between several topics you find interesting, such as comics and video games. In such a situation, you can be creative and create a website which is all about video games that are based on comics, or comics that are based on video games.

Once websites are built and are valuable, then they can be sold. Maybe you enjoy the process of creating a website, but you don't care about maintaining that website. If that is the case, then you can simply focus on your strength of creating a website which would be sold for money.

No matter what you do, this won't necessarily get easier. Most people don't have only one idea or interest. If you focus all your time and energy on one website that can be way too risky since you're putting all your eggs in one basket. Don't get to the point where the fear of failure paralyzes you from taking any action and trying anything. In this case, trying out different ideas can actually be a good strategy. Either way, you should focus on the smaller things you can do right now I since it will make starting to work a lot easier. The types of projects you should focus on initially are the ones that can be started quickly and finished quickly.

## Chapter 4: Online Business is Possible for Anyone

Once you have made a decision about your side project, then you are a lot more likely to go after it with more control without getting stuck. Financially, it makes a lot more sense going after your passion projects on the side while your main career is what is bringing in the regular income. This way, you can pursue your side projects without having to worry much.

You may be at the point of your life at which you are still thinking about launching an online business. You may be at that point, but you are held back by the worry of not having the necessary resources or skills. What this book is about is reminding you how all that is nonsense.

There isn't much difference between getting fit and running a business. Starting a business is one of those things that can make your life better all around if done properly. Just like getting fit, this is what a lot of people talk about, but they don't follow through more often than not. They will plan and prepare with no end in sight, just before dropping everything and returning back to the status quo.

In order to be successful at anything, it is necessary to have the drive, which is what makes plans into reality. This is something that anyone can do, but it all comes down to making a decision and realizing that there is no conceivable reason for you not to get what you are after.

The most common excuse for not doing anything is the fact that it takes money to start, which is not something everyone has just lying around. While there is truth to that, that is not enough of the reason to just postpone things and not to do anything.

The simple truth is that not every business requires a large investment. You could have your website up the same day for almost no cost. If you want to start getting visitors or selling goods and services online, you can start doing that really quickly. If you want to be a digital marketer, the only cost you really have to concern yourself with is the quite affordable web hosting.

If job security is something that's really important to you, you can keep it since none of the previously mentioned examples are do or die affairs. You can keep your job while working on your thing as long as you do it during your time off and during weekends.

Whatever the case may be, you want to get to the point where you can bootstrap successfully, which means being able to run the business from its own funds. To really make sure that this becomes a reality, you could first do something on the side which would guarantee you an income even though you may not like the activity itself. After you are sufficiently successful with that, you can use those funds to fuel your next side project which you intend to make into your main source of income eventually.

An alternative option is crowdfunding by using websites such as Kickstarter in order to earn money from anyone who is interested.

This goes back to having two categories of work to work with. There is a work which you love doing and which you would do even if it didnt pay a dime, and there is the work you do purely for money without much emotional investment. The brand you are working on during your off time does have its costs and expenses such as PPC and you need something which would pay for that, such as your job.

Another avenue would be providing a service online such as digital marketing. That is how real freedom is achieved. You can get the freedom and flexibility you need in order to create your dream lifestyle by performing SEO or any form or marketing for businesses. This is what allows you to create a schedule around the things which are important to you.

You may think that the lack of knowledge is what is holding you back. Most people still think that business is reserved only for serious-looking people in suits that graduated from a prestigious institution. That is also why a lot of people think that they won't be able to get far with their current amount of knowledge.

The truth is that all of the knowledge that you need is the one which can be gained naturally while working a job. Just start by creating your website, which should quickly propel you into learning what is important and what is not. For any other question, you can turn to resources such as books and consultants. Over time, if you stick with it, you will naturally gain more confidence and competence.

At the end of the day, you don't want to put all your eggs in one basket by focusing on just one venture. It is just not that simple. It will take time and effort for the things to start moving and you will need a more steady source of income until that starts happening.

So the plan is to have a main steady income source which sustains you until you manage to get to the point at which your side project becomes your main source of income. You know you are doing things properly if you are spending more time on things that you are passionate about and less on the things that you have to force yourself to do.

It is very important to start doing things as early as possible and to look into options that can enable you to earn passive income. In this way you are starting small and this is what helps you to buid up your confidence so that you could undertake larger projects which would really give you a good practice when it comes to your digital marketing skills.

If your first side project is a massive one which consists of creating a huge brand, then you will likely never get around to doing that since it will be very overwhelming and you won't have the belief that you can make it work. The fact is that it takes time for the benefits of this kind of goal to start coming in. It takes months and even years.

A lot of gurus preach about big, hairy, audacious goals, but a lot more reasonable approach is to start with something like selling an affiliate product. This is something you can start very easily and cheaply and you can also test things out quickly to see what works and what doesn't. The time and energy which you have to invest in this are minimal and even if things don't go according to plan, you will learn a lot based on that experience which will allow you to do better next time.

If you do end up achieving some success with this, you will have a source of income on the side, and that will make hitting you daily income goal a lot easier. This also means that you don't have to spend as much time working in order to get the money you need.

A business concept that is gaining popularity is the idea of failing fast. This may sound counterintuitive, but that is an approach which consists of building a minimally viable product and getting it out there so that real-world feedback could be acquired as soon as possible. The main goal of this approach is to get the product made as quickly as possible so that it could be put out into the world.

Doing things this way will be very beneficial for your mental and your financial health. What is truly soul-crushing is coming up with the perfect strategy and designing your funnel to a tee just for it not to take off, making all the time and effort that went into it worthless. If you want to create a funnel, create the basic funnel on the same day. If you notice that the funnel is working and that it is generating results, then you can refine it and spend more time on it.

## Chapter 5: How Much Time Does This Whole Process Require?

The thing that you probably want to know the most is how much time do you have to spend enduring at your job until your side project brings in enough income for you to quit? The news arent pretty and the truth is that it does take a while. If you, for example, want to build a mailing list which could ensure a good income from affiliate commissions, that takes time. Digital marketing, unlike what a lot of people may think, isn't something which would enable you to get wealthy overnight.

Digital marketing should be a tool which can be used to make money on the web as long as you are willing to do quality work and to market that work for a long time to come.

Creating a youtube channel which has grown to the point at which you can earn a job replacing income can take years. Most people can expect to be making a couple of hundred dollars per month in their first year creating Youtube videos. Building real traffic on the internet is hard work. You will need to be keenly aware of how frequently you have to post, how SEO should be conducted, and even if you are doing those things properly, it can still take months to have returning and reliable viewers.

Google AdSense is the program based on which Google shows the right ads to the right audience. The issue with AdSense is that is isn't enough by itself since you can only expect to earn a couple of cents per click. If you want any noteworthy income from this, you need thousands and thousands of views each and every day.

If you are not among people who are getting those kinds of views, you will need to supplement your income by offering an affiliate product or service. You can make good money with this, but the requirement for this is building the trust with your audience which isn't easy and it does take time. Trust can take years to build, but it can be broken in minutes. It is also helpful to utilize other forms of advertising such as banner ads, or other advertising platforms entirely.

If you want to improve your chances, you can also take advantage of influencer marketing. No matter what you do, these things take the investment of money and time in order to achieve noteworthy success, and it is necessary to be aware of this before diving in the internet marketing space.

## Chapter 6: Use Your Passion to Create Content

Internet marketing can lead to burnout if not having proper expectations. Decent passive income probably won't be as easy to earn as it may seem and, at first, you probably won't write about things you find passionate at first.

A perspective shift may be what will be required in order to regain motivation. You should start seeing yourself as a content creator. What you were doing all along hasn't changed, you are still building a brand and promoting it so that you could make a profit online.

If someone sees themselves as a content creator, then that person will focus on creating quality content and that is the key difference between content creator and an internet marketer. The quality of the content is dependent on many things, such as the logo and the content that is being shared. Someone who is taking content creating seriously is more likely to have an interest in media in general, which will improve the chances of the content being good.

When someone starts viewing themselves as a content creator, then that person will take the skills the skills that are necessary to create quality content a lot more seriously. Now the emphasis is placed upon creating something that people would want to see instead of just marketing a product or a service you don't necessarily stand behind.

When doing things in this manner, you will be more sought after and the work will be more enjoyable instead of being just a necessary evil for making money. It is so much easier to build a brand and to reach your audience quickly and effectively if your videos are crisp and of good quality. A lot of people are visual, and if you have developed an eye for graphic design, then it will be so much easier to create a WordPress website which would facilitate the selling of products and services.

People notice when content is created with passion and they will want to keep on reading such content. When Google algorithm notices the lower bounce rate on a website that is a host of good content, then that website is bound to be rewarded with a better ranking in the search engine. There are too many spammy internet marketers and that is why people who do things differently are in demand. Passion is important since you can still feel a sense of accomplishment and fulfillment even if your passion project isn't taking off at the speed you would want.

Someone who looks at digital marketing as something purely for making money is likely to put out subpar content and marketing the hell out of it and spamming people in an attempt to compensate for the lack of quality. Blogging with a certain amount of passion is far more effective for creating trust and thinking about the long term. If you think about your favorite things in life, those things were probably infused with passion, as opposed to something that was just churned out in an attempt to make some easy cash.

There is something that makes the blogs that are great stand apart from the ones that are subpar. If you save a certain blog as a bookmark, then that means that you want to see more of it. If you want for your blog to be a winner, then it is crucially important for you to be aware at all times about the things that separate quality from pretenders. The goal of the blog should be to keep people coming back for more and one of the most important elements of achieving that is writing with passion and starting from there.

Writing from the heart is crucial. Make a visit to a blog you like and read something there. If you pay attention, then you should notice that is that it seems like the writer speaks directly to you. You can also recognize the enthusiasm someone has when writing about the topic which is right for them. When these people write, they don't do it just for the money. They truly want to share their thoughts and feelings about a certain topic.

It is very easy to notice the difference between such genuine writing and something that is just looked up on wikipedia and rewritten just so that it could be put out there. There is nothing really new in this kind of content and no new value is created.If it sounds that the author of the posts doesn't care about them, then why should the readers care? The desire for writing about a certain topic should be there and if the motivation to write is just not there, then that may be a sign that it is time to switch topics.

If you are writing about something heartfully, then you are more likely to keep going even after you start wondering if you are doing things correctly and if your blog is headed in the right direction. You are less likely to throw in the towel after asking yourself if anyone is even paying attention to your blog and this is the only way you in which you can hope to work for the long term.

Things will get hard and you will not always be perfectly motivated no matter what your topic is, and at that point, it can be easy to start feeling burnt out if you don't really care about what you are writing about. Your chances for success are a lot higher if you write things for yourself because you find those things interesting.

Creativity is very important and it should be applied to each important element, such as the design of the site. It should look like the person behind it all truly cares because that is the only way in which other people could care. You have better chances if you are starting out with your own personal vision in mind instead of with something you saw someone else do.

When someone comes across your website, they should get the impression that they are looking at something unique and something that has its own flavor instead of something that was done many times over by many different people. When things are done this way, then you are increasing the chances that people will recognize the passions before they even start reading, and after that point, things tend to work themselves out organically.

It was always quite baffling to me when I would come across people who would focus all their energy on learning how to program some kind of content spinning software which would serve as a lazy substitute for building a quality website which people naturally gravitate to. This is only possible if you do what you love and if you do that for long enough, people are bound to notice eventually.

Your passions should also extend to the marketing aspect since you will need to do this a lot if you want to get your site noticed. This will be very easy if you are proud of your website and if you can't wait for an opportunity to talk about it. If the site isn't something you are exactly proud of, then you may not want for everyone to see it and you, therefore, won't put in as much effort in it.

# Chapter 7: How to Maintain Your Health and Happiness

If you do your work online, then you may consider your work to be pretty safe, unlike someone who is working on an oil platform in the middle of the sea. This line of work is not without its dangers, however, but these are a lot less obvious. Someone in digital marketing can get quite stressed out if certain things aren't handled correctly. If there is no awareness when it comes to certain things, then inconveniences such as weight gain and repetitive strain injury could happen.

It is very important to be aware of what you are getting in beforehand so that you are aware of the importance of taking care of yourself so that you could be viewed by other people as someone who has their stuff together instead of someone who looks for an easy way out so that they wouldn't have to do real work.

Also, if you don't pay enough attention to your health, you will find it difficult to do quality work and to ensure that the time you put into your work is time well spent. You are vastly improving your chances for success if you take a step back and take the time to keep yourself maintained.

If you are doing digital marketing, then there are a lof entrepreneurial aspects that come with that. Anyone who has had some experience with entrepreneurship will tell you that things are constantly going up and down. There will simply be days in which you are clearing out your to-do list like there's no tomorrow, while on other days nothing seems to go your way.

It is important to be mindful of health, both mental and physical if you want to last in this game. It will be very hard to do quality work if you are constantly on the edge of burnout.

First and foremost, you should know how to set boundaries between your work and your personal life. You should know when your phone is turned off and when no one can reach you. You should also separate your accounts so that your work doesn't bleed into your personal life and vice versa.

Meditation has been gaining a lot of popularity lately, and trying it out can have great benefits for you. When you meditate regularly, you learn how to do a lot better job at compartmentalizing things and being able to let go of things that don't matter in the moment and which aren't serving you.

You want to do the things which you love since you will get rid of a lot of unnecessary stress and pressure from your life. Stress over longer periods of time tends to wreak havoc with health. In order to get the stress under control, you should also have reasonable expectations so that you would fall into the trap of thinking that you would be earning millions in a year. You should try to enjoy the journey.

Taking care of your health doesn't have to be complicated and you can get plenty of benefits by just sticking to the basics. Anyone can make things complicated, but only a wise person can simplify things. You should focus on going to sleep on time. Your diet is a big part of your life and it should be given attention and consideration. Just make sure to eat less bad stuff and more healthy stuff. Being more active and exercising is also important since digital marketing jobs can be just as sedentary as regular desk jobs. Make sure to do some form of exercise each day.

When you can work from home, then you have the option of working in your lazy clothes and that can be tempting, although I don't recommend that since I find it impossible to be productive like that. Put some time into the appearance even though there may not be anyone looking.

The main point is that you should always have time for balance and for health since you can only stay out of balance and in the chaos for so long. If the balance is severely lacking, then you know that something has to be changed and tweaked.

# Chapter 8: How to Set Things up for Productivity

Looking after your health can take you far, but improvements in your productivity via your equipment and tech are also quite important and can increase your levels of happiness and fulfillment. Investing in quality gear is a very important piece of advice for anyone who is looking to get into digital marketing or online marketplace in general.

When you are in digital marketing, you can greatly increase your chances of success if you view yourself as a brand and as a business, even if you arent a traditional entrepreneur. Your passion is what fuels your product creation. The quality of the machine you are working on is very important because nothing kills motivation like long loading times or having to wait 5 minutes for the damn thing to boot up. The amount of time and sanity you would be saving by upgrading your machine would be invaluable.

The satisfaction of having a fast and responsive computer which does what you want and when you want is amazing. Work is hard enough and working on a piece of tech that works well improves the experience and makes it better. This improvement will be reflected in the quality of work and people will notice.

You need to take the time to create your home office. Working from home sounds awesome, and it can be, but it won't be for everyone since managing yourself and maintaining focus is really hard and will really challenge your discipline and your time management. When you are not at the traditional workplace, it is so much harder to do the work and procrastination tends to come in many shapes and sizes.

If you want to combat this, then you have to put in the effort to create your own home office which would prime you to focus and to get things done. Everyone is different and for a lot of people, traditional workplaces tend to be very distracting due to all the ringing phones and the fact that salespeople are put in the same room with the people who need silence to do their work. When you work from home, then you are able to design your home office in a way which would ensure your best personal productivity.

You will spend a good amount of time working no matter what you do and that is why it is necessary to make things as easy as possible for yourself. By doing this, you are more likely to be satisfied with your day to day life while also being reasonably productive with your work.

You should be willing to invest a little bit more into the design of your office since you will get a lot of returns on your initial investment if you get this part right. The best initial investment is a work desk since it has such an impact and is such a core component. The desk should fit nicely in your room and it should make you feel like the work you are doing is important. If you treat your work like it is important, then that will be reflected in the quality when the work is finished and out there for everyone to see.

To make sure that your desk is a good one, it should have enough compartments and there should be more space than you need so that you can be comfortable since it will be very hard to do your best work otherwise. If the desk has enough compartments for everything you need, then you will have everything you need at hand s reach and you won't need to get up needlessly. This makes you feel organized and that will prime your brain to be more productive and to work better.

You also want to make sure that there is sufficient space around your desk and this will enable you to place different work elements there such as more screens, filing cabinets and places for quick notes. A good desk should have all of these things, but if it doesn't, then you should make sure that everything that is necessary is within your arms reach.

You can handle several things at once when things are organized in such a manner. While you are writing something on a computer, all the relevant data you need should be close and easy to reach. As you work, thoughts and ideas will inevitably come up and you will need some kind of physical notepad in order to write these things down. When you are organized in this way so that you leave nothing to chance, you will inevitably feel professional and like someone who is doing something important enough. It is much easier to stay on top of things when everything is organized.

Notice board should also be a part of your office and this will serve as a place where you will pin things that are important and in this way, you can refocus yourself on things which are important and which add significantly to your bottom line without having to waste time and energy thinking about the ideal course of action.

You don't want to go too far and too close to the extreme by making your office minimalistic to the point that there isn't even an atom of distraction present. Simple things such as desk toys or some kind of music device can help you from getting distracted by far worse things such as social media and web surfing.

The chair is also an important component and you should make sure that the chair allows you to spin around so that you can reach anything you need around you without having to stop doing what you are doing. This all gives you an impression that you are in a serious work station which will give you an impression that you have everything you need in order to make things happen.

Home offices are all well and good, but if you want to improve your productivity and your happiness, you should get used to going to coffee shops. It is very important to break the monotony and to change the scenery when necessary since not many people can stand the same boring routine each day. What is interesting about coffee shops is the fact that people are watching and that is why you don't want to look like you are slacking, which is way too easy to do at home. Working at home can also be lonely, while at the coffee shop, there is a social aspect. Coffee shops are different than offices because you are unlikely to get interrupted as long as you look like you are working while still getting the benefit of the social aspect of the coffee shop.

# Chapter 9: Why be a Digital Nomad?

A digital nomad is something that has become reasonably achievable over the last couple of years. The ideal is achieving the freedom to travel and to have the independence of your time and your location, while relying on the income that is generated from your laptop.

Only things you need are the technologies, such as a laptop and an internet connection which enable you to set up a work station so that you could work from anywhere in the world. People who are on a really high level can do it all from their smartphone and as far as that is concerned, isn't that what a smartphone should be about?

Digital nomads travel around the world, making money online and using the advantage of cheap hostels which leaves them more money to do the fun and interesting stuff. You don't have to spend your whole working life in one soulless corporate building, you can take your laptop with you and see the world.

This seems to be the first thing most people think of when they hear about a digital marketing lifestyle. This lifestyle is pretty sweet, but it may not be for everyone and it is only one of many lifestyle design options. There are certain key points to consider before making a decision about a lifestyle.

If you want to be a digital nomad, then you have to be aware of the responsibilities that you have to take care of at your true home. Today's technology and infrastructure certainly give you an option of traveling an going to any place that is on a map, but if there are people in your life who don't have the option of being a digital nomad, then that may mean that you leave those people behind while you are away traveling. Most things in life come with a tradeoff.

Not everyone will be able to separate from friends and family for some time and this is harder for some people than for others. You can always travel with someone else, but it won't be easy finding someone who has either the digital nomad capabilities or the willingness to drop everything in order to travel with you.

If you are currently very cushy and comfortable, then you may have to be ready for not having access to those things for some time since you may have to stay at low-end hostels for weeks just to get by. If you enjoy tea every day, then you may not have that luxury in certain parts of the world.

Also, you will need to be aware of the logistics and the situation of the location you are traveling to since you may have to get your work station up and running if the situation calls for it.

Not everyone can manage to make a profit without a boss since not everyone has the discipline to make themselves do the work when it is necessary. Successful people do the things that have to be done no matter if they feel like doing them. This may be very hard to do when you are in a new city which you are tempted to explore.

The typical digital nomad lifestyle is just one avenue of changing your lifestyle. You can work online without necessarily traveling all over the place. Think long and hard what would make you happy and remember that people only show you only the good aspects of things on social media, while the fantasy isn't necessarily all that it is hyped up to be.

## Conclusion of Laptop Lifestyle

We've discussed an awful lot within this guide and explored some high-level ideas like side hustles, work-life balance, prioritizing workloads and productivity techniques. Now let's summarize everything we've found out.

In case you are an online entrepreneur or a small business at that point you are going to most likely frequently feel as if your assets are being stretched to the point where you're failing to get all things done. Odds are you are going to be juggling several projects at once and attempting to decide which of your various obligations or side projects ought to come first.

For example, if you utilized bootstrapping to finance some of your bigger projects, then that is going to imply you may have to offer services regularly so as to keep your funding. Iin case you're doing that then you are going to also wish to see to it that you, in fact, spend some of your time going after those projects that you're more enthusiastic about too and that might possibly be more lucrative in the long run. But then you have to pick which of those ventures to devote the most time to, and which to do initially, all while accomplishing different administrative activities and handling the additional drains on your time.

The trick to all of this is to understand what you desire from life and the way in which your online business fits into this. Do you desire a totally passive income which enables you to travel and ignore work? Or are you delighted to work hard indefinitely, provided that it's on a subject that you relish?

More notably, how much cash do you require to live? What are your personal ambitions? How much time is it going to take you to make that money? What are the different factors you could work with to obtain the lifestyle you desire?

Additionally, think about what you require to get your online business going. With all that said, you could then figure out how much cash you have to make and see to it that you do that daily. Be meticulous and leave time for yourself and for your passion ventures.

In case you're something like me, then you are going to most likely have around 20 side projects taking place at any one time in addition to your primary 'job' and other obligations. This is something which was acknowledged at the company I worked for last where they claimed to work utilizing the following criteria: family first, then work, then personal development.

The family first thing is something which's vital to keep in mind once you're an entrepreneur, as you don't wish to get so entangled in striving for success that you neglect the main reason you wished to be triumphant to begin with, which was most likely to spend more time with your loved ones and to be in a position to provide for them.

Work then takes place before development (which could imply personal development or R&D), since you have committed to your employers and clients the moment you undertake these jobs and producing outcomes on time is essential for your credibility and your ongoing financial stability.

The threat here is that you may wind up never really getting round to the tasks which you wish to deal with and so fall short to make any progress as a business since you are going to be too occupied meeting your day-to-day requirements.

To fix this issue, a good system to utilize is to divide your workload into particular segments which you are able to then work through in sequence. For example, you may assign the initial half of your day to your promptly pressing duties and the obligations you have to clients. Following this, you may then separate the following half of the day into administrative work followed by work on your ventures.

This would imply that you are going to certainly get time to deal with your projects, however on slow days or times when you have a substantial workload, your most vital duties won't be the ones to suffer. You would then additionally draw the line beneath your day as soon as you had accomplished that to mark the conclusion of your workday and to prevent it spilling over into your personal life, your family is going to thank you and you are going to enter into work with more vitality and invigorated enthusiasm.

To determine which of your projects you wish to prioritize, it may be beneficial to carry out a bit of math and to explore your forecasted time-to-completion against the possible profit of the project. Simply put, then, in case you have a long project which is something of a labor of love for you, you might wish to de-prioritize this and concentrate on the shorter and more promptly lucrative tasks.

In case you accomplish the smaller tasks initially and these begin generating profits, then you'll boost your overall turnover a lot more rapidly than you would working on an extensive and uncertain project at first. Once you have accumulated some success and expertise, you can, at that point, turn your focus to the more enthusiastic concepts.

Naturally, though there is regularly the possibility that if one of your tinier side projects blasts off in too big a way, it might wind up stopping you from ever concentrating on your dream projects. While profits are vital, it's just as important to see to it that any tasks you spend time on suit your firm's mission statement. In case you can't get enthusiastic about it, then it's not worth accomplishing it.

So for the burned-out blogger or the online marketing nut, here are a few measures to taking pleasure in a higher quality work-life balance:

Develop a business model with steady income flow and a passion undertaking.

Understand accurately how much you have to make to finance your way of life and your passion ventures. Furthermore, understand the lifestyle you wish to live and think about a digital marketing approach to attain that.

This may imply transforming into a digital nomad, but think it through thoroughly. Make that amount daily, then shift focus.

Deal with one side project at once. See to it is a thing which you love doing. See to it is a thing with a desirable risk/reward ratio.

Begin with fail-fast, tinier business projects to learn and to begin producing more passive income. Do not devote months and months on a sales funnel for your initial project.

Slowly change the focus from the grind to those passion ventures. Develop several revenue streams.

Take care of your physical and psychological health. Maintain the psychological discipline to stay clear of the urge to keep working and to divide your life and work.

Meditation may be very helpful.

Eat, sleep, work out.

Dress for the job you desire!

Invest in yourself: in an excellent home office and a wonderful, strong pc for doing the work.

Visit coffee shops to get away from your personal environment.

You are able to travel more without essentially turning into a digital nomad!

Discover the passion. Turn into a content creator beyond just a marketer.

Don't count on overnight success, get rid of the pressure!

This implies writing a rigorous routine to specify when you focus on which projects, in addition to when you'll complete work. And this is what ALL of this truly boils down to, and that is discipline. With discipline and enthusiasm, you are going to manage to overcome this enormous monster and make digital marketing work for you. Everything is achievable!

I hope that you enjoyed reading through this book and that you have found it useful. If you want to share your thoughts on this book, you can do so by leaving a review on the Amazon page. Have a great rest of the day.